ARCHAEOLOGY: INTRODUCTORY GUIDE FOR CLASSROOM AND FIELD

Ellis E. McDowell-Loudan

State University of New York College at Cortland

Prentice
Hall

UPPER SADDLE RIVER, NEW JERSEY 07458

Library of Congress Cataloging-in-Publication Data

McDowell-Loudan, Ellis E.
    Archaeology: introductory guide for classroom and field / Ellis E. McDowell-Loudan.
      p. cm.
    Includes bibliographical references and index.
    ISBN 0-13-090844-4
      1. Archaeology—Methodology.   2. Archaeology—Field work.
    3. Archaeology—Handbooks, manuals, etc.   I. Title.

CC75 .M38 2001
930.1—dc21   2001036902

VP, Editorial director: Laura Pearson
AVP, Publisher: Nancy Roberts
Editorial assistant: Lee Peterson
Marketing manager: Chris Barker
Editorial/production supervision: Kari Callaghan Mazzola
Prepress and manufacturing buyer: Ben Smith
Electronic page makeup: Kari Callaghan Mazzola and John P. Mazzola
Interior design: John P. Mazzola
Cover director: Jayne Conte
Cover design: Kiwi Design
Cover photo: Ellis E. McDowell-Loudan

This book was set in 10/12 Palatino by Big Sky Composition
and was printed and bound by Courier Companies, Inc.
The cover was printed by Phoenix Color Corp.

© 2002 by Pearson Education, Inc.
Upper Saddle River, New Jersey 07458

Printed in the United States of America
10 9 8 7 6 5 4 3 2 1

ISBN 0-13-090844-4

Pearson Education LTD., London
Pearson Education Australia PTY, Limited, Sydney
Pearson Education Singapore, Pte. Ltd
Pearson Education North Asia Ltd, Hong Kong
Pearson Education Canada, Ltd., Toronto
Pearson Educación de Mexico, S.A. de C.V.
Pearson Education—Japan, Tokyo
Pearson Education Malaysia, Pte. Ltd
Pearson Education, Upper Saddle River, New Jersey

To my husband, Gary L. Loudan,
and my two children, Suzanne V. McDowell Lyon and James C. McDowell

CONTENTS

PREFACE

THE DEVELOPMENT OF A TEXTBOOK REQUIRES EXTENSIVE PLANNING AND MANY revisions. Even then, those who read it may think of better ways of saying what the writer wished to convey. Ideally, when this happens, those readers will jot down their reactions and comments and give them to the author for consideration in later editions or in follow-up efforts. Or, an instructor might use the book as a starting point for lectures that offer a different viewpoint.

In some cases, reactions to an author's efforts reflect the reader's or author's background, the type of research utilized within the text, or the diverse regional situations illustrated by the examples provided. Whatever the case, comments, suggestions, and reactions—both positive and negative—are healthy. They stimulate thought and should promote and encourage critical thinking and debate.

To be successful, any textbook should generate some sort of reaction and discussion. Sometimes what the author hopes to convey will be the source of this response. Other times, topics peripheral to the author's focus will accomplish this. Any feedback to points raised by a text is useful. While some comments or criticisms may be inaccurate, requiring correction or clarification, others may be both accurate and vital as indicators of points needing further study. Nothing could be more healthy than open-minded consideration of these factors, and it is my hope that *Archaeology: Introductory Guide for Classroom and Field* will inspire such consideration!

I would like to thank the numerous people who have contributed to the development of this textbook. Family members, teachers, colleagues, students, editors, and friends have offered their ideas and suggestions. All of these people have helped mold the final product. Without them, the book could not have been written. In addition, I would like to thank the following reviewers, who provided helpful suggestions: Thomas H. Charlton, University of Iowa; Curtis W. Marean, SUNY Stony Brook; T. Patrick Culbert, University of Arizona; Robert D. Leonard, University of New Mexico; and Francis B. Harrold, University of Texas at Arlington.

Ellis E. McDowell-Loudan

INTRODUCTION

AS A STARTING POINT FOR A BOOK THAT INTRODUCES READERS TO A TOPIC, WE shall begin with a series of questions. First, what is it that you like about archaeology and why did you decide to study it? Is it because archaeology consists of sensational and remarkable discoveries in far away places? Do you envision studying remains of early settlers in your region? Perhaps you found bits of old crockery or odd pieces of corroded metal in your yard that do not resemble anything you use today, and were excited about what they imply about previous residents.

Has there been a controversial new shopping mall built in your home town, which caused the demolition of a popular playground or an intriguing old house? Were archaeologists called in to carry out a study before the mall was built? Did they find some amazing clues to ways the land had been used long before your town developed? Sometimes when this happens, the archaeologists involved provide programs for the local historical society. Did you happen to attend one of these and get inspired to learn more about archaeology?

Once there is an exciting archaeological find, there may be a stream of telephone calls and letters arriving at the newspaper, television, historical society, or local college inquiring about updates or offering similar types of information. Sometimes this leads to further discoveries. Occasionally, as a result of this type of publicity, new archaeological sites or collections of artifacts are reported to someone who was involved in the archaeological project. Perhaps you heard about some of these types of discoveries and their aftermath, and want to be part of the exploration and future excitement!

Usually it is the mysterious and unusual find and not the commonplace discoveries that spur interest and publicity. These are the events that we hear

1

the most about, and in some areas, these reports are followed by other reports from other areas because the newspapers or other media recognize public interest in them. When a number of these events are reported in quick succession, readers and viewers may get the impression that there is a steady stream of captivating discoveries, all the time. It is this expectation of constant discovery that draws many people to archaeology.

Truly, there are pieces of our heritage all around us. However, many times these clues to the past are scattered, disrupted by more recent activities, or viewed as too commonplace for much attention to be paid to them. Much depends upon the area, the current interests of people in those regions, the potential for their destruction, and the prospects for funding study of them.

Local, state, and national centennial or bicentennial celebrations are examples of events that tend to trigger increased interest in the history of particular locations. It is at those times that publicity may increase, funding may become available, and numerous projects, including archaeological ones, appear. These tend to generate publicity, publications, and increased community interest. Perhaps such an event has taken place recently in your town, and has sparked your interest in archaeology.

Are these the reasons you decided to study archaeology at this time in your life? Perhaps they are part of the explanation. Other reasons may be more practical. Perhaps a course in archaeology fit a school requirement and your schedule. However, with many options available, you probably weighed the subject matter against that of other courses to help you reach a decision.

Still other reasons may be deeply personal. For example, you may have become interested in archaeology because you were disturbed about the loss of a special site in your home town. Maybe this stimulus has sparked an interest in a career in archaeological—or cultural—resource management or protection! A desire to know what to say, how to say it, and how to argue convincingly for the protection of human heritage in the world may be your justification. Or you may believe that becoming an archaeologist might be a thrilling career choice.

A preliminary question raised by many people, especially students and their parents, has to do with career choices and the best training for them. What do you do with a degree in archaeology? To me, the answer is exciting. Archaeology is part of anthropology, the study of people and their cultures, past and present. We are becoming an increasingly global society, and what could be more relevant in this day of interaction with people from all over the world than to learn all we can about ourselves and our ancestors? When looked at that way, it is clear that this branch of the social and behavioral sciences, as part of a liberal arts education, is a useful direction to take.

To be more specific, a person with a bachelor's degree in anthropology, with an emphasis in archaeology, is a person with a broad educational background. Jobs that specify a bachelor's degree are open to you. If you want a career with more emphasis on the archaeology part of your training and interests, advanced degrees such as a master's degree or a Ph.D. may be useful to you eventually. On the way to those goals, though, there are opportunities for you to gain field and laboratory training and experience—chances to acquire a wide range of knowledge, insight, and "seasoning."

FIGURE I-1
*Ruins of a plantation house near the Smithsonian Environmental
Research Center, Ann Arundel County, Maryland.
Note the wall thickness, fireplaces, bricks, and chimneys.*

FIGURE I-2
*At Grindstone Island, New York, remnants of cut stone in an abandoned granite quarry
are clues to an important late-nineteenth-century industry on the island.*

Sometimes field and laboratory experience will count toward college
(academic) credit; occasionally there is the chance to find paid employment,
even as an undergraduate student, if you have taken an archaeological field
school course, laboratory course, or museum-study course, or if you have
participated in some sort of internship program that offers these types of experiences. While many of the initial jobs will be relatively low-paying, they
tend to open doors to more lucrative opportunities if you are enterprising
and hardworking. Often, when these jobs are connected to colleges and universities, there are incremental raises and advances in the levels of employment and experience. There may be opportunities to defray costs of graduate
work. When the jobs are connected to private contracting companies, there
may be similar options, and possibly grants or scholarships to further your
training academically—and professionally.

What are some of the job options? After a season of field school training,
you may find work as an archaeological crew member, or possibly as a crew
chief, helping to supervise other archaeological crew members. Instructional
and interpersonal relations skills, as well as knowledge of computers, photography, mapping, drawing, botany, geology, zoology, chemistry, or other
areas, may lead to added options within archaeology or peripheral to it.

Writing skills, managerial aptitude, and knowledge of or interest in environmental law may lead to other potential career directions.

Thus, when asked what may be done with a career in archaeology, I offer the following preliminary list:

1. Teaching and museum work—All levels are possible, depending on interest and educational degree and certification obtained; age levels for your focus of training may be a factor.
2. Peace Corps or Student Conservation Association—Various levels, places, interests, and skills are available.
3. Excavation—As noted previously, this often is connected with cultural resource management and contract archaeology projects; levels are dependent on training, experience, and area of the country or world; it may include participation in major research projects in locations like Africa's Olduvai Gorge or Hadar Region, Turkey's tell sites, Italy's classical sites, Latin America's Mayan, Aztec, or Inkan (Incan) areas, or North America's Mesa Verde, Chaco Canyon, Cahokia, or Jamestown sites, or California's Spanish Mission sites.
4. Environmental law—Often this area is connected with contract archaeology and cultural resource management; jobs may be found in local, state, and federal agencies and may require some of the general tests they offer for levels of job placement; legal training may be an offshoot of combined interests in archaeology and laws relating to it.
5. Forensics—The application of training and skills from archaeology, anatomy, physiology, and criminology may lead to this specialization; jobs tend to be connected with local, state, or federal agencies.
6. National Park Service—Various levels and places available that involve different interests and skills; governmental testing may be part of the placement process; park resource management, park curation, supervision of staff as well as site rescue and stabilization after forest fires, floods, or other disasters, are potential job responsibilities.
7. Historical societies—All levels of training and interest in historic and prehistoric human activities, curation training, museology, and other skills may be needed.
8. Tourism—This could involve training for tour-leading to visit various archaeological sites around the world and working with various international organizations; often a range of foreign language skills is essential; additionally, some of the recreation and tourism programs in academic settings may be needed or desirable.

These are some of the potential directions to explore if you are interested in an eventual career in archaeology. Other directions are as varied as your imagination. You may be an exceptional writer of grant proposals, nonfiction articles and books, or fiction with an archaeological focus or theme.

Sometimes there are jobs available with magazines, publishing companies, governmental organizations, local chambers of commerce, and other agencies for a person with combined expertise in writing and archaeology. By now, you may have other ideas that are not listed and you may want to visit your school's guidance or career planning and placement office to seek out other possibilities! Do it!

WHAT IS ARCHAEOLOGY?

WHAT IS ARCHAEOLOGY? STATED SIMPLY, IT IS THE STUDY OF PAST HUMAN LIFE. It is not the study of ancient dinosaurs, old fossils, buried bones, or funny-looking stones, unless these have some connection with human beings. Often, archaeology is defined as "the study of ancient ruins or ancient people." While this is true, the "ancient" part of the definition is misleading. Any people of the past may be the focus of study—whether they are the earliest human ancestors who lived six or more million years ago, or recent people who lived a couple of generations ago. Indeed, some archaeologists study "other people's garbage" in contemporary society. (More will be said about this later.) "Ruins" as part of the definition also may be deceiving. While some sites have remnants of structures that are visible, many other sites are less obvious. The study of the past, then, requires diverse approaches that suit particular situations, people, and environmental contexts.

In the Introduction, archaeology was referred to as a subdiscipline of anthropology, within the social and behavioral sciences. This traditional framework puts emphasis on human behavior and the cultural context, or setting, in which the behavior occurs. Attempting to reconstruct the larger picture of societies and their structure, function, and history is an essential goal of archaeology when viewed this way. (However, a focus on the environment and the manner in which people, sometimes very small groups of people, use, affect, and are affected by it, tends to be a significant consideration at initial stages of the study of an archaeological site, a community, a neighborhood, or a region.)

In the United States, archaeologists tend to be trained as anthropologists first and specialists in archaeology second. This perspective has led to the term *anthropological archaeologist* for professionals in that field. In Chapter 8, you will see differing opinions on that approach, but this text will offer guidelines for "doing archaeology" from the anthropological archaeologist's point of view. As a brief guide to supplement and reinforce a field director's or instructor's introductory lectures about field work, this book may be helpful as backup or reinforcement for the lectures and for the early field experiences. Perhaps it will help students formulate questions that come to mind during lectures. However, a book is no substitute for archaeological field experience.

Anthropology is the science, or study, of human beings and their patterns of learned behavior. Anthropologists study people; these people may be our contemporaries or they may be ancient people who lived many years ago. "Patterns of learned behavior" refers to all the ways we human beings do things—the way we react to events, eat, sleep, dress, work, play, study, and interact with others, as well as the beliefs that direct what we do and how we do it. Although all people share some basic behavior patterns, each society—each culture—is distinguished from others by the particular configurations, or sets of patterns, that direct what they do, what they do not do, and how they do and do not do things. Some of these configurations are so subtle that "outsiders" to a culture will not recognize them and may be offended by certain behaviors.

Each object made, modified, or used by human beings reflects the learning accomplished by the user and maker of the object. This does not mean that the user knows how to make the object, or that the maker actually uses his or her creation, at least not in our kinds of technologically complex societies! If you consider any object in your view at this moment, for example, it represents diverse types of knowledge and skills needed to make it and use it, particular choices you or others have made to select it, and various purposes for its presence where it is located and how it turned up where it is at present. Any of your possessions may be viewed this way. Listing all of an object's characteristics, all its uses, its "history" (where you got it, when, why, and how, for instance), illustrates the type of orientation an anthropologist may have when contemplating an object. Archaeologists call all these objects *artifacts*. When the object is studied as an example of human behavior and all the implications that relate to that context, the artifact represents the *material culture* of the maker and user. As the term suggests, material culture is a visible manifestation, or example, of how certain human beings do things.

When an object (artifact) is "old" and represents human beings of the past, often we know very little about it—at least, we know very little about the object from our own first-hand experience with it. In this case, comparing the unfamiliar item to an item (artifact) that is familiar to us may not be dependable as a method for identifying an unknown object. The object may generate more questions than answers. Further, if we view it exclusively from your prospective or mine, without attempting to break from the cultural patterns that direct our ways of describing and understanding an object, then our explanation of it—our identification of it—may be wrong! Anthropologists refer to using prior knowledge of one's own culture to define a similar-looking object from another culture as *ethnographic analogy*. While that may be a valid starting point, it may mislead us. Sometimes, it may be informative to inspect the ways modern descendants of the makers and users of the objects utilize them—or to inquire how they believe their ancestors may have used an artifact, as a helpful means of identifying its form, function and use, and its meaning to the people. Although this application of oral tradition ("My grandparents used these objects to do X.") may be useful, it is not always completely accurate. Times change and so do customs and the explanations of them.

With these definitions, distinctions, cautions, and other remarks in mind, what is anthropological archaeology? It is the study of human beings and their ways of behaving as represented by the objects and structures left behind, as well as the environmental settings (locations or contexts) in which these things are found. This is the simplest way to begin to define what the term means, and, as in the case of any object we use (and often take for granted) today, there is far more to what this means than these words convey! Perhaps the remainder of the book will help broaden the definition and explain anthropological archaeology more clearly.

Experiment   Select any object and make a list of all the information about it that you can. Even in the case of the "simplest" objects, there will be parts of its nature that you recognize but probably could not define in scientific terms. However, you know where you could find that type of information.

Discussion   If you choose this book as your object you know that it consists of paper of different grades, specialized techniques for binding and gluing, colors of printer's ink, the printing itself, the language in which it was printed and all the rules of grammar and semantics involved in the vocabulary it utilizes, the route the book took from its manufacturer to your hands, and all the features resulting from today's technology that resulted in its form. Many of these factors are unimportant to you when your goal is to read it. However, the history of paper, the technological experimentation and competition between publishing companies to provide their product in the most attractive form, and the scientific knowledge and skills required to produce the book are extremely important if the "book" is an "object of study," an artifact, an example of the material remains of our culture. Not only that, but the subject matter itself reflects views contemporary with the publication. These views may be different from outlooks previous to, or long after publication!

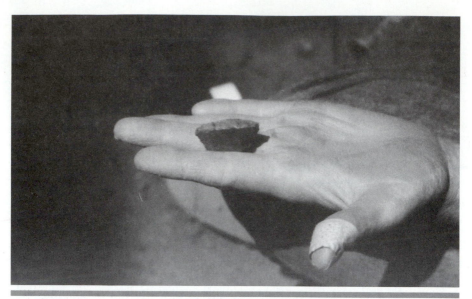

FIGURE 1-1
Stone artifact with a steeply chipped edge—possibly it was used for scraping animal skins.

FIGURE 1-2
Diverse land use along a river valley in West Virginia's
Ridge and Valley Province illustrates human behavior.

FIGURE 1-3
An urban example of diverse land use in Shepherdstown, West Virginia, differs markedly from rural examples of land use.

FIGURE 1-4
Remnants of a limestone-processing kiln, Engle Switch, West Virginia.

Only a sample of some commonly used methods, theories, and questions will be presented in this text because our purpose is to introduce the subject matter and to provide a relatively brief, general survey. More detailed textbooks, and more specialized ones, are available if you wish to explore archaeology in greater depth. You might want to refer to the Dushkin/McGraw Hill *Annual Editions in Archaeology*, popular journals such as *Archaeology, Smithsonian, Natural History, National Geographic*, or *Discover*. Professional journals like *American Antiquity, Man in the Northeast*, and *Journal of Field Archaeology*, and textbooks emphasizing particular regions of the world, like R. J. Dent's *Chesapeake Prehistory*, or B. M. Fagan's *Ancient North America: The Archaeology of a Continent*, or his *World Prehistory: A Brief Introduction*, offer added depth. These and other examples are provided in the bibliography. The Internet is a wonderful source for special topics. Sometimes it is helpful to begin with the Web site for journals specializing in the area of your interest. Other times, you will have better success if you use one of the search engines like Yahoo or Infoseek, and follow their directions to explore the topic of interest. The goal of this book is to present some frequently asked questions and provide some answers to them. Maybe the questions and answers will serve as "teasers" to encourage you to investigate further.

Let's look at some of the questions focused on in this book, and some preliminary answers:

1. What is archaeology?
2. How do we do archaeology?
3. How do we know where to dig?
4. How do we know how deep to dig?

WHAT IS ARCHAEOLOGY?

From the previous discussion, it may be clear that the definition of archaeology is elusive. It cannot be understood from one sentence. So far, the concept has been placed within an academic discipline—anthropology. Popular definitions found in pocket dictionaries were presented and embellished. A few common misconceptions were noted (archaeology doesn't study stones, bones, and fossils willy-nilly).

Archaeology is an orientation—a way of looking at the world around you to see what people do, how they do it, where they do it, and why they do it. People and their patterns of learned behavior are the focus. Admittedly, the clues to people and their behavior tend to be whatever bits and pieces of debris (ruins, garbage, etc.) they have left behind them. For the most part, people of the past are emphasized in an archaeological study, although sometimes "the past" isn't very long ago.

Indeed, some archaeological studies look at today's trash. An example of this type of study is done by William Rathje and his colleagues (Rathje 1979, 1991; Rathje and McCarthy 1977; Rathje and Murphy 1992). Their emphasis is on the information gleaned from modern refuse. They study the hypothesized regularity and variability of some American cultural activities today, comparing what people say they do to what their refuse shows they really do.

This type of study demonstrates what we do and do not know about ourselves. Often, what we think we do or how we believe we behave differs from what the (archaeological) evidence may show. For example, we may believe we are economical in our choices of particular types of foods. Recovery and analysis of our garbage may demonstrate that we have wasted or discarded much more because we chose cheaper varieties. When a cheap cut of meat is purchased, for example, a reason for the lower price may be that there is more waste bone, gristle, and fat. Often the novice cook does not know this, assumes all meat is alike, and finds out the resultant, penny-pinching, culinary masterpiece is, in at least her or his view, inedible.

Sometimes an archaeological study of a recent site results in an inaccurate interpretation, when it is based solely on clues left in the ground. If it is possible to confer with those who "created" the site, it may be feasible to correct the errors in interpretation. Brian Fagan and F. Van Noten discussed a Zambian site, Gwisho Springs, where excellent preservation of plant remains from the site showed available food resources 4,000 years old (Fagan and Van Noten 1971). Conferring with modern Zambian "hunters" from the area, the researchers were able to demonstrate that the modern Zambians continued to utilize the same vegetal materials as their predecessors, although in both cases the people themselves had been referred to as "hunters."

Further, the !Kung San of the Kalahari Desert in South Africa—so-called "classic" hunter-gatherers—once were portrayed by outsiders, and by the San themselves, as people dependent on the males' hunting prowess for survival. Some researchers perceived these hunting activities as continuous and time-consuming. Study of actual subsistence patterns has shown that the majority of the San diet consists of plant foods gathered by the women (Lee 1979). Shostak describes this in *Nisa: The Life and Words of a !Kung Woman*: "!Kung women contribute the majority (from 60 to 80 percent by weight) of the total food consumed. Averaging little more than two days a week in the quest for food, they gather from among 105 species of wild plant foods, including nuts, beans, bulbs and roots, leafy greens, tree resin, berries, and an assortment of other vegetables and fruits (Shostak 1981, 12)."

Perhaps this portrayal is less romantic and dramatic than the dauntless hunter fighting furiously to feed the family. The misconception possibly reflects early-twentieth-century-male, Western European-based value systems in which males were the heads of households—the so-called "breadwinners." Since the majority of early anthropologists and anthropological archaeologists were males, they were most likely to focus on what males did and how males perceived their role in society. Also, many nonfarming societies, including South African ones, refer to themselves as people who hunt. Without additional probing, the value of meat could be magnified, while the reality of the true diet could be misunderstood.

Bones tend to be larger and to be preserved in archaeological sites better than vegetal remains. In analysis of archaeological materials found in a site, presence of giraffe, antelope, or other animal bones in the refuse might be viewed as support of the importance of these species to the society. These bones tend to be larger than any plant remnants; bone size alone could magnify the importance of animal species—especially when the preconceived notion of the importance of animals to the diet is present.

FIGURE 1-5
Catoctin Furnace, Maryland, 1778–1905.

On the other hand, it is important to recognize another aspect of this type of interpretation. The late Harvey C. Moore, professor and department chair at American University in Washington, D.C., related his experiences, and those of his wife, Sarah, with the Dine (Navajo) of the southwestern United States. Their research occurred in the aftermath of the federal government's stock-reduction projects that were devised to decrease herds of horses and sheep so that the so-called "over-grazing" in the arid southwest could be counteracted. Although the project seemed valid on paper and in government offices in Washington, the government policy appears to have disregarded the major importance of these animals to the Dine as a source of food, as a way to acquire wealth, as a means of trade and exchange, as well as symbols of community interaction such as sharing, and inheritance. The Moores, during their stay in the southwest, were told repeatedly when visiting Dine families that the people were hungry for meat and missed having adequate mutton to eat. This was a continuing indicator of the sense of loss caused by the traumatic stock-reduction policy of the U.S. federal government in previous years. As you can see, people's perspectives on various topics and activities differ.

Experiment   *Think of an activity that you consider to be extremely time-consuming, and write down your estimate of how much time you devote to it. Measure the actual number of hours or minutes you spend on the activity the next time you do it. Does the amount of time you measured correspond with your estimate? Are there "extenuating circumstances" that you think altered the accuracy of your estimate this particular time? Are there other daily activities, like eating, sleeping, or dressing, that take up a large proportion of your time, but which do not seem to do so because you enjoy doing them more or do them somewhat unconsciously? Compare your calculations with similar behaviors of roommates or friends to see how they correlate.*

Discussion   *This experiment is an example of the manner in which archaeologists try to look at people and their actions. Each of us perceives what is or should be the behavior of others or ourselves in a unique manner. Because of this, we may ignore or overlook the "reality" of our behavior. By applying a technique like this to something familiar, we may gain insight into what might be overlooked when studying the unfamiliar.*

Archaeology is also the study of the objects that people made, modified, or used. These may be large or small (toys, clothing, utensils, carts, automobiles), portable or fixed (tools, stone fireplaces, castles, the Sphinx, Easter Island statues). These objects are called artifacts. Artifacts are studied to gather information about who made them, how they made them, and why they made them. How, when, where, and why the objects were used are other questions archaeologists try to answer. The term applied to artifacts when they are studied in this manner is material culture. Since artifacts are the most long-lasting clues to human behavior, they provide the majority of evidence an archaeologist has available for reconstructing past societies. As in the case of the differences in preservation of bones or plant remains in a site, large, nonperishable artifacts, like stone tools or pottery, will survive better than woven cloth, baskets, wooden objects, feathers, or other perishable artifacts. Therefore, what we find is not the complete picture of what was left behind, what the people who lived in a place had, used, liked best, or treasured most. Making matters even worse, places where people lived long ago may be the same spots used by people today. What remains after new folks clear, sweep, move, reuse, or burn will limit what can be learned about earlier inhabitants of the area.

Thus people, places, human-made objects, and the reflected or suspected activities of people are basic ingredients of archaeological study. Viewing the world around you from the standpoint of how a site was used, what it looked like when it was being used, what features were used at those times as landmarks, and what the site's limitations may have been, requires caution and imagination! These, too, are factors important to an archaeologist. A site or potential site must be evaluated on the basis of what it looks like today, what aspects may have changed, and which ones may have remained constant. This approach permits application of any number of research questions ranging from the ones relating to the identity of the people, to those aimed at determining what their relationships were to one another, to the land, to resources present or missing, or to the people's interrelationships with neighboring human populations.

Having looked at many definitions and examples of archaeology, we are now in a better position to summarize an answer to the question "what *is* archaeology?" It is a set of specialized techniques and perspectives for learning about people (ourselves) and their (our) patterns of learned behavior. Relationships between environmental features (rivers, hills, swamps, gorges, volcanoes, oceans, deserts, and forests, for example) and human activity areas (villages, camps, cities, fishing or hunting grounds, gardens, factories, walled compounds, for example) are studied. These relationships are called *archaeological context*. The locations where clues to human activities are found are called *archaeological sites*. Although there may be many villages, camps, fishing spots, gardens, factories, or other sites, no two sites are identical. Each archaeological site, like every human being, is unique. Archaeology is also the study of objects found in a site. Every artifact tells something about its maker or user. Evidence of a skilled or novice craftsperson, meticulous or careless maker, or even left or righthanded use may be visible. This added reminder of our individuality as human beings underlines the remarkable uniqueness of our species.

FIGURE 1-6
Sorting lithic (stone) artifacts.

FIGURE 1-7
Settlement pattern today.

HOW DO WE DO ARCHAEOLOGY?

From the definition of archaeology you may have guessed that there are many ways to approach the study of people of the past. You know that people are found in diverse places, with unique settings. Evidence may be on today's ground surface or deeply buried beneath many layers of soil and rock, or the evidence may be of even more recent human behavior. Each context will require a special strategy to get the most information from it.

For example, if an archaeological site lies beneath a lake or reservoir, a number of highly specialized and "water-customized" approaches are required. Scuba gear (including tanks and other needed items for deeper, longer-term dives), underwater camera equipment, special lighting, and equipment developed specifically for marking locations under water will be needed. A boat will probably be necessary, with equipment for guarding the scuba divers, storing, preparing, and repairing their equipment, as well as all the lines used to transport materials from the site to the boat. No doubt, there will be video cameras and a direct communication system between the divers and the boat. This list ignores many of the essential aspects of this type of archaeology, called *underwater* or *marine archaeology*. As is the case with land-based study, underwater archaeology varies markedly by site nature—sunken ship, flooded village—locality, water depth and temperature, salt water versus fresh water, types and severity of currents, and political jurisdiction. In rivers within the United States, the U.S. Army Corps of Engineers supervises any underwater research. International waters where shipwrecks may be encountered often require negotiations with nations whose ships are involved. Within the limits of waters claimed by various countries, other legal arrangements are required. There are many specialized books and articles on this type of archaeology; this text will focus on land-based archaeology.

The chapters that follow offer an array of examples of how archaeology is done. There are other ways that have not been included, so do not assume that the entire range of possibilities has been tapped. Because each human being is different from every other, and because each archaeological site is distinct from others, approaches must be geared to the situation, as well as to the available techniques.

HOW DO WE KNOW WHERE TO DIG?

Facetiously, the answer is "we use a crystal ball." Others say "educated guessing" provides the answers. Today, there are innumerable nonintrusive means of improving upon guesswork. Often referred to as *remote-sensing devices*, these relatively new technological approaches offer added ways in which to conduct archaeological research with less emphasis on digging.

Aerial photographs of many kinds and qualities are available. What do they provide and how might they illustrate remote-sensing? From the air, ground disturbances may be visible that cannot be detected while standing on the ground. For instance, the Peruvian *pampa* area contains the famous Nasca Lines that were not noticed until the 1930s when commercial airplane travel across the Andes Mountains led to their discovery (Aveni 2000). Photographs of these amazing earth and stone patterns continue to mystify and fascinate researchers.

FIGURE 1-8
Aerial photographs without a plane.

FIGURE 1-9
Aerial photograph of Ruppert Island, Maryland (18 MO 26 Site).

Various types of equipment are on the market for use in the search for buried materials. Unfortunately, most of the equipment is expensive, it becomes outdated very rapidly, and it tends to be geared to certain types of buried material. In particular, many of these devices are most useful for locating buried structures, like walls, pyramids, and ancient canal beds. While their value cannot be denied, it would be difficult to justify the expenditure of time and money to utilize these tools if the focus was on the location of a series of small campsites, scatters of stones, bones, or wood debris from the individualized efforts of one person or one family's activities within a section of a river valley. This is true in particular when there have been numerous, more recent uses of this same area by other people, doing other things. Distinguishing which subsurficial concentrations were relevant to which time period and cultural group would be virtually impossible through this means alone!

Metal detectors, some of them quite inexpensive, may be useful as a guide to buried metals. Indeed, some are sophisticated enough to filter out modern debris (cans, pop-tops, or aluminum foil, for instance) and may even indicate the depth at which particular types of metal objects are located. Using these may enable researchers to locate areas in which there are concentrations of materials that may be of significance to their study. These locations could be marked to reflect spots that registered on the metal detector so that they can be tested using controlled archaeological excavating methodology. However, if the research interest is based on cultural groups without metal in their artifactual assemblages, metal detectors are without value for site location. They might be informative as a supplement to other remote-sensing devices, though. If the sites of interest, found through use of other remote-sensing equipment, are tested with a metal detector, the *absence* of metals registered by the metal detector might be encouraging.

Various types of ground-penetrating radar equipment, magnetometers, and electromagnetic sounding equipment, initially developed for military and mining use, have become important as nonintrusive tools for archaeologists. In almost all instances, these are extremely expensive and may or may not prove useful for particular archaeological studies. Many large-scale, government-sponsored projects utilize these tools today. For the most part, they are informative when the project area is multiacre rather than when it consists of small campsites or scattered settlements. A stimulating and informative set of articles in the *Annual Editions Archaeology 00/01* (Hasten 2001) offers a cross section of some of these techniques and their applications around the world. An exciting success story of how these devices may save vast amounts of time and fruitless effort is the Ceren Site (Sheets 1992). This remarkable site in El Salvador was buried abruptly and completely by volcanic eruptions. Through use of remote-sensing devices, it has been possible for researchers to plot where particular types of structures are located and what their relationships to one another might be. Referred to by some as the "American Pompeii," the Ceren Site is an excellent example of the value of the new technology.

If you are disappointed to learn that digging, or *excavation*, is not the first step, or even the most important step, in archaeology, perhaps learning why this is the case and what some of the alternatives are will ease your disillusionment. Probably, one reason so many people expect archaeology to mean digging is that most reports in the media announce, describe, and photograph sites that have been excavated or are being excavated. These announcements are attention-grabbing and they make it appear as if, through some mysterious means, the researchers knew instantly where to dig to get the answers to questions they wanted to answer. All the preliminaries are glossed over, and only the more flashy and sensational parts of the project are presented.

Sometimes digging is not part of the archaeological study at all. If a set of archaeological sites has been excavated previously along the shores of a river within the boundaries of known tribal territory, for instance, the archaeological research questions may be (1) Where did the people in this territory find the clay they used for making pottery? (2) Is there an area within the territory where these people could quarry the stone (or *lithics*) they used for fashioning tools? (3) Where did they fish for all the fish earlier researchers discovered in their trash *middens* (piles or dumps)? If the society was known to have depended on farming or herding of domesticated animals, perhaps the research question will concern location and measurement of appropriate farm lands for raising food for people and farm animals. In the situations described earlier, would you jump out of the field vehicle and start digging? Without some evaluation of all that has been done previously and all the information available already, mere digging would serve no purpose.

The archaeological strategy would be to review all the information noted by all earlier researchers in that area. Their studies may have emphasized other things, but their maps, background descriptions, and reports of finds, as well as the bibliographies cited by these researchers, may save you from retracing their steps. Sources of information you may find helpful include data gathered by geologists, botanists, zoologists, and even hydrologists, meteorologists, agronomists, local farmers, historians, and construction personnel! Certainly, if there are any living descendants of the earlier human group, they would be primary informants to consult. Using any of these sources, you could begin to create a model of the ecological relationships of the people within their territory. This approach may lead to questions that require test excavation in parts of the territory previously ignored, but that is not necessarily the case. As you can see, excavation isn't the only, or primary, or first source of answers to archaeological questions.

Study of climate, prevailing winds, seasonal variations in temperature or rainfall, danger of flooding, and danger of drought may be significant. How the inhabitants used their environment and what difficulties they might have encountered may indicate where excavation might be most informative.

In locations where no living descendants are available to help, and where no subsurface testing (excavation) has occurred, and where an archaeologist predicts there may be evidence to document a research question of concern, controlled digging (*subsurface sampling*) may be planned. Where to excavate is based on clues discovered on the ground surface, logical "best guesses" based on topography of the area, or a systematic approach to the area of interest. In frequently flooded areas, a place with a slightly raised elevation might be a focus, the assumption being that low spots might have been scoured by flooding over the years or that those using the area would be more likely to choose a (high) dry spot. Because this would be a guess, using today's logic based on today's appearance of the landscape, often a sampling of the area would include both high and low spots. Frequently, the test excavations would be carried out in a random pattern in an attempt to overcome the biases of our preconceived notions of what people of the past might have done and where they would have done it. At the same time, though, it is unlikely there will be storage pits, fire hearths, or other activity areas where it can be documented that an area was never dry land.

Sometimes artifacts lie on today's ground surface. In arid regions where there is little vegetation, wind and occasional violent downpours may wash

FIGURE 1-10
Light-colored spots only indicate red sandstone bedrock close to the surface causing differential growth of vegetation in Piedmont Plateau, Maryland.

FIGURE 1-11
*Rocks mark a fish trap remnant, V-shaped, extending
from shore to shore, and always under water.*

out objects that previously were deeply buried. A dramatic example of this phenomenon occurs in some of the major East African sites where our earliest ancestors have been found—Ethiopia's Hadar Region and Tanzania's Laetoli and Olduvai Gorge. Each year, after the annual monsoon season (when it comes), paleoanthropologists return to these localities to see what fossil fragments have been washed out of the eroding hills and gullies. It is in these areas that the Leakeys and other researchers have found some of our most sensational hominid (human) fossil bones.

In cultivated fields, plowing, followed by rainstorms, may expose objects. Road, water line, and house foundation construction may unearth objects. Rodent activities—skunks digging for grubs, groundhogs excavating holes—may result in exposure of artifacts. Based on these surface clues, the archaeologist may design an excavation plan to explore what may be buried in the vicinity.

Sometimes the choice of areas to test is based on the nature of the location. If there are clear boundaries—a small rock shelter, a narrow strip of shoreline bounded by water on one side and rocky cliffs on the other three sides—testing options may be limited. Along with these restrictions, there is still more to consider. How did residents get to the rock shelter or shoreline? Is the rock shelter one of several in close association with one another, or is it truly isolated from any others? Is the shoreline eroding or expanding (due to changes in water levels or tides, for example)? If water levels have risen over the past few hundred—or thousand—years, perhaps much of the site lies beneath the water; possibly, all that will remain will be an edge of what had been a much larger site.

It is unusual, today, for any archaeological project to excavate an entire site. A rock shelter, for example, may be tested or *sampled* through excavation of a section, to determine what, if anything, may be present below today's surface. If the sample reveals deeply buried artifacts or features, such as fire pits, storage pits, pottery, burned bones, stone structures, or other evidence, these must be evaluated and their spatial and cultural relationships must be considered. Results of these analyses may suggest the likelihood that more information is present in specific parts of the site. This helps direct the next step in the study of the site. If, on the other hand, no cultural materials are found in the initial test excavations, researchers may conclude that the rock shelter was not used by people, or that the sampling choice was faulty and neglected the right sections of the shelter, or that more tests are necessary. In the case of a rock shelter, often a fire hearth is located near the opening, to direct the smoke outward, resulting in charring of the ceiling in this area. Other activities—sleeping, food-preparation, tool-repair— may have been carried out farther into the rock shelter. However, since natural light may have been useful for some activities, the area in front of the

FIGURE 1-12
Rain-washed cultivated field shows exposed stone material in central New York.

shelter may have been the focus of some activities. If the rock shelter has a steep slope (talus) in front of it, and if the shelter has been utilized for more than an overnight stay, or by several groups on several occasions, users may have swept rubbish out of the shelter and down the slope. Where to dig and how deep to dig in each of these areas may require careful consideration in each instance. Each *locus*, or separate area, may be distinctive in its potential as a source of information about the people who used the site.

Another consideration will be the archaeologist's research interests. A focus on the development of cities would require study and excavation in regions of the world where previous research showed that extensive farmlands, water supplies, forests, and other natural resources might have supported city growth. In some cases, especially in regions of the world where there are limited water resources or a dependency on irrigation to facilitate farming, village and more recent city sites may have been constructed, refurbished, and reconstructed one on top of the other. These moundlike phenomena, consisting of rubble from the earlier settlements, are referred to as *tells*. Often, they are located in regions where surrounding terrain is quite flat. An example of a tell is Jericho, located near Jerusalem. Subsurface testing of a complex tell site would require a different strategy and a larger research team than excavation of a rock shelter. Where to dig would depend upon which time of occupation, or occupations, are of interest, how much *overburden* (wind-blown ground cover) is present, and how much of what types of rubble are present. Again *locational analysis*, that is, the study of the relationships of the tell to water supplies, roads for travel and trade networks, sources of fuel, food supplies, and other necessities, would guide choice of areas of this complex site of interest to the archaeologist. As is the case in any type of research project, it is essential to learn as much as possible about the nature of the site, and this tell site, specifically, before deciding what portion would be sampled. Undoubtedly, remote-sensing equipment would be used as part of the preliminary study strategy.

An interest in how the European ceramics found in a 1700s Haudenosaunee (Iroquois) settlement contrasted with the European ceramics found in a contemporary Dutch settlement along the Hudson River would require intensive study of maps of New Netherlands and its historic settlements, as well as study of the trade partnerships and other relationships that provided access to these ceramics. Again, where to dig, if digging is to occur at all, might be determined by the history of settlement of the area, previous studies that have been done, and information available in various European centers, particularly those where the ceramics were manufactured. Often, records from the pottery or china manufacturers and exporters include detailed inventories of objects sold and shipped overseas. However, these data may be mere hints of the routes by which specific objects reached their final resting places in a specific archaeological site.

As we have seen, surface clues brought to the attention of an archaeologist may be part of the decision-making process when planning to study a particular topic in a specific locality. Sometimes artifacts are discovered on the surface of a freshly plowed field or in a newly excavated trench for a pipeline or drainage ditch. These objects may be shown to an archaeologist in the area and may result in the landowner and archaeologist arranging for some site exploration before additional destruction of the site takes place. The surface indications may or may not reflect where in the vicinity the actual settlement or activity area is.

Closer inspection of the ground surface in a tract of land may reveal clues of significance to the researcher. Broken pieces of pottery eroding out of a groundhog hole or stream bank, for instance, may hint that there could be a village, camp, or refuse pit in the vicinity. Irregular land surfaces, in otherwise level countryside, may hint at a buried settlement. Unusual vegetation patterns, sometimes visible only from an airplane, or from the top of a hill, may indicate where people have camped, built something, or buried something. Remember, these factors may or may not relate to the particular research questions of interest to the archaeologist. Often, it is difficult to distinguish the age or affiliation of outlines of previous structures or differences in vegetation growth patterns.

A practical consideration when deciding where to dig is access. If research interests require travel abroad, visas and permits to work in an area are dependent on the country's laws and restrictions on foreigners. Also, this

FIGURE 1-13
Rope outlines burned soil that proved to be a buried smoking/roasting pit.

type of research is more costly in time and money than domestic research, and will be dependent to some extent on political factors. For example, in 1997, American archaeologists were prohibited from working in Iraq due to the political situation. At the time this book was being written, some areas of the Balkans continued to be off-limits to archaeological researchers from the United States. While this is most important to the archaeological project director, it is of concern to anyone who hopes to participate in archaeology elsewhere in the world. Many project reports omit these details, leading the uninitiated to expect an enthusiastic and open-armed welcome if they go to "do archaeology" elsewhere in the world. In some cases, there is an ignorance, perhaps an *ethnocentrism*, in the outlook of those who believe they would be doing another country a favor by helping them dig up their heritage. In my view, it is a disservice to prospective archaeologists of tomorrow if we do not mention that we are guests when we go to other countries. We are not the only ones with knowledge and skills for doing archaeology, and we are not the primary specialists on those nations' histories. I believe it is of benefit for the novice to recognize potential stumbling blocks in their field of choice! Some of these possible limits may be continuing responses to earlier unsatisfactory interactions between those nations and your predecessors. We take with us our notions of the best way to carry out research; indigenous people may perceive these notions as inappropriate, presumptuous, or even sacrilegious. Respect, diplomacy, and open-minded approaches are essential if success in these situations is to prevail.

To conclude the discussion of how we know where to dig, we shall look at one of the most unsettling experiences for the beginning archaeology student: The field director does not know exactly what will be found in an archaeological site—or where it will be found (or even *whether* it will be found). While this lends an atmosphere of mystery and anticipation, it can seem disorganized and time-wasting, and may even suggest "leadership ignorance!" Indeed, this stage of archaeological research makes students uneasy ("Why don't I know what to expect?") and project directors edgy ("What if we don't find anything despite my best guesses?"). This situation also makes some project directors wildly speculative and melodramatic in their efforts to maintain a high level of enthusiasm and anticipation in the new field crew. However, despite the best efforts of archaeological research and preparation, and no matter how many years a researcher has expended in working at particular sites or regions, sometimes the most promising locations yield nothing!

This underlines an essential truth: Every archaeological site is unique. Because of this, each site must be treated in the manner best suited to what its attributes reveal to the archaeologist. When you remember that every event in your life is also unique in certain respects, it makes the archaeological situation less surprising, since archaeological sites and their contents are remnants of human behavior—clues to events in people's lives at a particular time and place—just like your life and its events.

Experiment   *If you live in a dormitory where rooms have the same dimensions and are provided with the same basic furniture, make an inventory of two or three (superficially) to see how they differ—carpets, damage to furniture, covers, curtains, use of electrical outlets, or other accouterments. Compare and contrast areas within the rooms where one room has objects and another has nothing. Diagram these rooms and their contents, to scale. Then, place lines equidistant from one another parallel to and then perpendicular to one another (that is, create a grid). Do all the vacant squares correspond in all the rooms? Are there some squares with distinctive contents? These variants illustrate human diversity and human creativity, don't they! Also, if there are some squares in your grid that have nothing in them except bare flooring, these could be equated with some of the excavation units in any "real" archaeological site—where nothing is located!*

How Do We Know How Deep to Dig?

At first, this seems like a simple enough question. A site ought to have a bottom to it, one assumes. However, some places have been used or visited only once by people, and may have only a thin layer, or *stratum* (plural, *strata*), of things left behind by the human users of the site. In other places, people may have used the site over and over again, piling up new deposits of debris, one layer on top of another, and sometimes digging holes into earlier layers. Since you do not know what sort of situation exists in a site, the depth of excavation may vary a great deal.

Sometimes, the determination of how deep to dig depends on other considerations. How much horizontal area is part of the land used by the people of the past at this location? How many excavators do you have in your crew? How much time is available for the excavation? What particular information would you like to gain from the research? Will it be possible to return to the site at a future time to continue work on it, or must everything be done immediately with no chance for added excavation? If only one chance to study the site is possible, probably the most useful plan is to excavate a small horizontal area to the deepest stratum with any clues to human activity. Of course, you could argue that gaining information from one time period through a wider excavation would be valuable. However, there might be no opportunity to learn whether there are more deeply buried cultural strata present at the site. In either case, there will be a loss of data if the project is rushed in this manner.

If the research concerns use of a particular site at one particular time, by one specific group of people, excavation is likely to be carried out in a manner that will expose that period of usage—that *living floor*. Probably, this approach will consist of test excavation, which opens up a set of adjacent squares, or *units*, to provide horizontal exposure of features that contain artifacts relating to that time of site occupation.

In Figure 1-13 (on page 26), a discoloration found on today's ground surface in a plowed field was visible after a rain. It was marked with a rope and pieces of fire-altered stone (burned, discolored, and shattered into brittle chunks) were plotted within this segment of the field. The density of these stones was much greater than similar finds elsewhere in the field. This same area had registered increased magnetic intensity when the magnetometer was used. Sampling of some units within this area revealed the buried pit feature shown in Figure 1-15 (on page 30).

In Figure 1-9 (on page 19), an aerial photograph shows an island in the Potomac River with evidence of many rock outcroppings protruding from the river. Close study of the aerial photographs of the island, known as Ruppert Island, suggested that erosion may have down-cut areas between these stones, eventually separating the island from the mainland. At the center of the island, there is a slightly raised area, consisting of numerous layers, or strata, of flood-deposited silt. While picnicking on the island, a woman and her son discovered a projectile point. Recognizing the significance of her find, the woman reported the artifact to the Archaeology Society of Maryland. After initial exploration of the island, Archaeology Society members contacted American University in Washington, D.C. The following year, under the direction of Dr. Charles W. McNett Jr., with my assistance, the site was excavated formally and my master's thesis reported the findings (McDowell 1968).

FIGURE 1-14
Prehistoric artifact found 30 cm. (12 in.) below today's ground surface—excavation did not yield any evidence of more deeply buried cultural strata.

FIGURE 1-15
Shallowly buried burned area, partially truncated by plowing.
This burned pit was located beneath the discoloration shown in Figure 1-13.

FIGURE 1-16
Mapping a living floor with wide exposure in Ruppert Island, Maryland.

Figure 1-16 (on page 30) shows an area of ex~~p~~
mapped (foreground) and the stratigraphy be.

If the research concerns the sequence of ev~~~~
time, excavation of squares or units may incl
earlier, followed by deeper vertical excavation tl
and expose older living floors or occupation are

Naturally, there cannot be culturally stratified ε
did not leave behind any preserved clues to activiι
than one time. If people only used the site one time,   ...ι
of the set of events that the archaeological excavators   ..ιtter how
deep they dig! However, if the excavations do not exten   ,, ueeper than a particular living floor or set of cultural debris in the horizontal exposure, there
may be no way of knowing whether there are other buried clues to earlier
human behavior at the site. As a result, in most cases, archaeologists try to excavate at least some portions of their sites until they reach bedrock, glacial
gravel (determined geologically to be the basal limit of any cultural activity in
the Americas, at least from our current viewpoint), or a stratum of impenetra-
ble clay judged to be undisturbed by human activities. In this manner, they
document the full complement of human activities represented at the site—or
at least at the sections of the site that have been tested.

FIGURE 1-17
Deeply burned cultural materials are indicated by dark bands of strata.
There are small fire pits at the base of the excavation.

FIGURE 1-18
Excavation of flood-deposited strata at Smithfield Beach, Pennsylvania, has a deeper test pit (sounding) in one excavation unit to check for buried cultural features.

FIGURE 1-19
A test unit was excavated to determine whether buried cultural materials were present; only glacially deposited gravels were found in central New York.

Why would an archaeologist bother to excavate a site more deeply than is essential to the research question? One reason is that perhaps this will be the only time excavation at this site is possible. If some effort is not expended to determine the cultural information that may be present in the site, there may be no second chance. Another reason is that once the site is excavated, it is destroyed. It cannot be put back together as it was before excavation. Although it may be possible to stabilize the site so that extensions of excavations could occur in the future, damage done through the initial excavations may create erosion, change drainage or percolation of ground water into deeper levels, or generate other damage to more deeply buried strata. Therefore, often at least a sample of the deeper strata will be tested for future reference and for assurance that something will be recorded.

Since the researchers do not know what they will find until they find it, sometimes they encounter types of archaeological resources that are not familiar to them or do not fit their expertise. For example, if I were excavating and encountered a generator or part of a large industrial complex, it would be essential to stop working and contact specialists with knowledge of those types of structures. Otherwise, I might destroy the clues to context or damage the structures themselves. No one is an expert in every type of human behavior and all kinds of material culture! Ironically, on occasion this problem has worked in reverse. In some sites, there are cultural strata that are considered "too recent" to be significant. In these cases, some researchers may dig through these strata to reach those of concern to them. Needless to say, this is destructive and may cause irrevocable damage to or loss of cultural resources. These data may be of interest and importance to other researchers. Also, of course, the information from those times and localities may represent vitally significant portions of human history necessary for a true picture of cultural continuity in the area. Careless disregard for any part of our past may result in historic gaps. Therefore, in most instances today, archaeologists examine and record all cultural materials and strata encountered during excavation.

Despite these factors, there are some basic strategies used on sites in any geographic area. These will be described in later chapters as will some of the alternative approaches used by some archaeologists. Each archaeologist brings a personal bias to the selection of research and student training. The ones presented here reflect a frequently revised set in use today for some central New York State sites. However, these same strategies have been used or observed in many other regions.

CHAPTER

2

Bringing Out Your
Inner Archaeologist

THE CHRONIC COMPLAINT OF INTRODUCTORY ARCHAEOLOGY STUDENTS IS THAT they read and read, pore over pictures, and *still* do not know how to do archaeology or how it feels to do it. Probably, no book is ever going to solve this problem or relieve this frustration to the classroom-bound student. Some schools and museums have devised artificial sites—sandbox-like structures—for simulated archaeological experiences. In some cases these are indoors; elsewhere, they are constructed in school yards. Although this may provide some of the excitement and mystery of archaeological study, its artificiality detracts from it. A problem with such projects is that carelessness or unthinking haste destroys the site or some part of it, but "no harm is done." In an actual archaeological excavation, there is no second chance—if the excavations are treated thoughtlessly or carelessly, information is lost. Also, there is at least a tendency for students to assume that any "real site" they encounter will have plenty of materials in it for them to discover and record. When a simulated site is constructed, artifacts, or items that represent artifacts, are installed; various types of features may be manufactured to provide a wider range of things to find and document. Indeed, in such a situation, everything will be on a small scale, and there will be things to find and document—probably in close proximity to one another. This gives students the sense that positive archaeological results ought to be quick and easy! Additionally, if a modern-day archaeologist creates the simulated site, it will reflect modern ideas or notions about the "culture" it represents.

Fortunately, there are real sites to visit, museum reconstructions to look at, and archaeological field schools in which to participate, if the student desires to do so. These may satisfy most students with genuine interest in an archaeological field experience. In some cases, taking part in an archaeological field school shows the student that other aspects of the study of human beings, past and present, are of more interest. An article in *The Arizona Republic* reported on a paleoanthropology field school, directed by Arizona State University Professor Kaye Reed (Go 2000). This field school works with the Institute of Human Origins, cosponsored by the University of Witswatersrand in South Africa. Reed commented that students either love or hate the experience, and learn through this adventure whether they want to pursue a career in that field.

Sometimes, the technology used for doing archaeology will be of more interest to the individual—perhaps the test-manufacture of various artifacts, known as *experimental archaeology*, will be the new direction taken by the student. Others may determine that their interests lie in chemical analyses of soils to distinguish and identify animal and plant organic remains, trace element analysis of pottery or stone to locate sources exploited by earlier site users, or studies of astronomy to help correlate site orientations, uses, and structures with the summer and winter solstices or other astronomical features.

Frequently, field school participants are students from other disciplines. Initially, some students from other fields fear they lack some vital information already in the hands and heads of their fellow students who have an anthropology background. While there may be some terminology that is helpful, and perhaps there are some insights or perspectives that have been gained in other anthropology courses, all first-time field school students are in line for a new experience. Also, students from other disciplines will contribute additional knowledge and offer a perspective different from that of the anthropology student. The student of history may contribute information about important events and locations as background to the study of the site. Biology students with plant or animal anatomy and lifestyle knowledge, may "see" these features of the site more rapidly than others. The geology student may be first to recognize soil types, features of water-transported rock or soil, glacial remnants, or stone types. The health science student may be fascinated by the potential values of particular herbs, or concerned about the health risks that were confronted by earlier site users. An avid hunter, fisherman, or hiker may note features of the topography, animal trails, and spots on rivers and lakes that are prime for their interests, before these are recognized by others. Each participant will contribute a refreshingly unique perspective!

Fears of demonstrating ignorance, concern for getting a good grade, and general worry that a major mistake will demolish the project because of information known to "everyone except me," confront most beginning field school participants. Here is a secret, however: You know many more things about the "basics" of archaeology than you realize! This is not a license to be heedless or careless. However, almost everyone played in a sandbox when they were young, or poked around a gravel pile, or perhaps made sand castles at the beach. Do you remember how moist sand held its shape, while dry sand did not? Do you recall dribbling very wet sand through your fingers to make towers for sand castles? Have you ever seen an anthill, with its neat cone of sand and central entry hole?

You may have done a bit of gardening, either outdoors or in flower pots. Can you visualize the soils with roots in them and how they were often more porous than those without roots? Do you remember how much harder it was to dig a hole in compact clay soils than in topsoil that was loamy and filled with organic matter? Did you ever water the plants only to find that the water would run off the compact clay but it would be absorbed easily by looser soils? Did you ever sift the soil through your fingers to remove stones, roots, and other debris? If so, you are aware of textures and visible factors that are relevant to any kind of excavation.

Some plants do better in one soil than in another, as the avid gardener or nursery specialist is eager to explain to you. Often gardeners add fertilizer along with richer soil, peat moss, or something else to improve or change soil conditions. No doubt you did this, too, or perhaps you purchased a bag of "potting soil" or "cactus soil." You may have observed (possibly subconsciously) how this changes the color, texture, and nutritional makeup of the garden, at least on a small, temporary level.

Most gardeners discover that their little garden patch is far larger than they originally thought when the time comes to dig and weed it. Where to put the garden for best results may be a problem, too. You want adequate drainage, sun, level terrain, and the best soil conditions. However, the plot must be convenient, not in the pathway you or others use, and possibly, protected from the activities of wild or farm animals. This may mean fencing, and probably means consultation with others in your family or community.

How do your gardening or early sandbox experiences fit into the archaeological picture? First, they indicate that you are at least vaguely familiar, at first-hand, with the "feel" of soils of several kinds—even if sandboxes and packaged potting soil are the maximal limits of your experience. Second, these experiences show that you are aware of soil variation when wet or dry. These experiences also show that you have prepared layers of such materials—soils, wet and dry sands, or fertilizers—seeing the color and texture variations these may create. Finally, these experiences show that you have gained a knowledge of location considerations. Perhaps you have been instructed not to put your garden or flower pot in particular locations because they block window access or will be trampled—or you observed these things for yourself as you figured out where to position your project.

Selection of a place to excavate is based on many of these same "common sense criteria." Certainly, being careful not to bite off more than you can chew as far as size and area, and taking into account your time, strength, and inclination to complete a project are important considerations. It is also important to recognize factors that may have affected where earlier people did things that may be apparent to you because of your earlier experiences. If

FIGURE 2-1
Here experimental burning of pottery made with different clays and temper
or binding material (like sand, gravel, or shell) added to clay is shown.

there is one, and only one access route through a gully from a hilltop to a stream, it is logical—in your view as well as that of earlier trail-users—that this would have been the path taken. Naturally, any previous hiking experiences you may have had will lead you to rule out the idea of climbing down the cliff on a rope!

Another similarity between your gardening experiences and archaeological field work that could be useful is that digging, for whatever purpose, may become tedious. This is the case whether one wants a well-cultivated garden or an excavated archaeological site. Insects tend to descend on the hapless digger; vegetation roots appear to multiply, making digging more difficult, equipment causes blisters, and the returns for the energy expended seem meager. Then, as is the case in archaeology, the excavated plot may not produce well. Surface indications of good, deep, rich soils (or scattered archaeological remains) may not reflect what is buried beneath the surface.

To complete the analogy, soils that have had something added—organic or inorganic commercial fertilizers or human and other garbage—behave somewhat differently from those that lack these additives. The result, in either gardening or archaeological research, may be differences in quantity, variety, or lushness of vegetation. These variations may or may not inform you of something useful for your purposes.

On farms, there are often buried remnants of older outbuildings. Sometimes these areas include discarded building debris, manure, animal carcasses, and other materials that have been swept into the old foundation. While hiking you may have seen sites like this. Perhaps you may have wondered whose farm it was, when it was abandoned, and why. When these sites are found, there may or may not be any record of them. Therefore, they must be excavated carefully and documented meticulously. Debris swept into such ruins may include prehistoric artifacts. Attempting to reconstruct where the fill came from and whether there might be undisturbed prehistoric sites nearby often results in testing in adjacent areas. Figure 2-2 shows an example of this type of discovery. Exploration of surrounding areas revealed a number of similar localities, but no evidence of an undisturbed prehistoric site.

So, the "inexperienced" student has these bits of basic knowledge and experience to bring to bear on the readings or the excavations in archaeology. You truly possess a fund of insights waiting to be tapped within an archaeological context!

FIGURE 2-2
*Old house foundation rubble may contain
earlier cultural debris.*

FIGURE 2-3
Here is a modern picnic site on Grindstone Island, New York.
What will be found years later?

Other experiences, virtually unrelated to archaeological training *per se*, can prove useful in an archaeological context. For example, the arrangement of furniture and other possessions in your bedroom—what do you put where, close to what, and why—or the condition of a campsite or picnic area before and after use. What is present when you leave a room, campsite, or picnic area, and what does it tell about diet, technology, packaging, numbers of users, or duration of use of the area? Are you able to distinguish, or make a good guess about, the gender of the site users? Will debris left by one person be completely different from that left by a group? Archaeologists look for and study just this type of "happening" when they are excavating a site. A *habitation level* refers to the scattered clutter of bits and pieces of human and natural debris from approximately one time and one locale, left by one person or by a group.

Similarities between archaeologically detected materials and your own clutter are quite feasible—consider how you behave at a picnic. Where do you stand or sit? Do you trample some of the grass or weeds, or leave prints in soft soil or mud? Where do you cook? How do you dispose of garbage? How do you put out your fire? Did you ever look at the spot you used weeks or months later after it has been rained or snowed on, or has had other users? What of its "history" does it still reveal? What does not remain? Are there indicators that birds, rodents, or other types of wildlife have visited the site since you

FIGURE 2-4
*Here are the only remains of a prehistoric campfire on Ruppert Island, Maryland.
Charcoal and other organic materials have been washed away through flooding.*

were there? What might this suggest about the types of disturbance you would
find in any or all archaeological contexts?

Again, you know, or intuit, far more than you *know* you know! Con-
sciousness of these kinds of things are part of archaeological sensitivity. Experiment with this approach. It can be informative, enlightening, and even
amazing!

Experiment   *After you have eaten a meal and have cleared away the remnants,
look around the space—floor, table, chair, sink, stove, fridge, trash can, and so forth—
to see remaining evidence. A crumb, fragment of napkin, wet streak where you wiped
the table, footprint in water by the sink from when you washed your hands—all of these
are clues, and all are familiar to you today. Are any of these potential clues to look for
in an older archaeological context?*

*Figure 2-4 is an example of a prehistoric campfire. Unfortunately, it was found
deeply buried in flood-deposited river silt. All the charcoal and other organic materials were gone. Only the stones remained as tantalizing clues to an event from
long ago.*

How Do We Know Where to Dig?

URING OR FOLLOWING SURFACE STUDY, THE RESEARCHERS PLAN THEIR STRATEGY for subsurface testing, usually with frequent reference back to notes and maps. The landowner may be an invaluable source of information about what has been found there previously, where it was found, and what else may have been done to the site. Other factors that must be considered are barriers to excavation, such as buildings, fences, driveways, trees, grape arbors, paved areas, or spots where discarded equipment has been abandoned. Sometimes these obstacles can be moved. On other occasions they may limit choices of excavation locations. Probably, you will want to note reasons why an area is omitted.

Our major concern here, though, is how do we know where to dig? Further, how do we decide how large an area must be excavated in order to accomplish what is needed to answer our research question? These are difficult questions to answer! An archaeological site in any area, large or small, where people have been or have done something, is unique! Clues include unnatural-looking ground surfaces, burned areas, or objects and structures visible on the surface. For the most part, the particular human activities of interest to an archaeological team will be limited to certain types of people at a particular time or period of time. However, when inspecting a potential site, any evidence of any type of human behavior should be recorded. That means the archaeologist notes glass, paper, cigarette butts, corn refuse, seed or fertilizer and their bags, grease or oil and other discharges from motorized vehicles, as well as clues more likely to represent the times and cultures of interest to the research project. Any and all of these types of things could have modified what is buried beneath them.

Archaeologists do not want to make mistakes in judgment when selecting areas to test. Not only will the excavated soils be disturbed, but so will areas around the excavations. Walking or driving back and forth to the areas under study, putting down supplies and equipment near excavations, screening (sifting) soils from the excavations (referred to as the *backdirt*), all the other kinds of occurrences that may transpire by chance or design, will make an impact on the landscape near the work area. Since these things change the appearance of the area and may disrupt what is below the surface, it is important to scrutinize the ground surface carefully when selecting places to test.

If there are clues to cultural behavior that are not relevant to the research project, but that might be significant for other research, it is not ethical or smart to disregard cultural evidence just because it is too recent or not significant to the current study. An example common in rural areas where farming continues, would be ignoring an old barn foundation or using it as a convenient place to pile equipment or backdirt. Studies by other researchers might determine that the barn had historic significance for the development of early farming in the area. Further, as your research progresses, it might become evident that a better understanding of how plowing had been done in the past was important. Study of the barn and the human behavior it reflects might clarify how deeply earlier plowing had gone into the soils, what sorts of crops might have modified the organic content of the soils, and whether there had been localities within or adjacent to your excavations used for manure dumping!

FIGURE 3-1
Note the barriers to excavation on a college campus.

FIGURE 3-2
Archaeological excavations may be required indoors, for example, when unexpected discoveries are made during installation of an elevator shaft. Remnants of an early-nineteenth-century burying ground were found beneath an elementary school in Homer, New York.

FIGURE 3-3
An eroded river bank revealed Native American pottery sherds (fragments) and oyster shell exposed along its edge at Swan Point Neck, Maryland.

Observing what today's farm machinery does and how it may modify the area is enlightening, too. Figure 3-4 shows a machine planting seed, fertilizer, and weed-deterrent adjacent to the excavation. Other machinery may weed between the corn rows and at some point during the early part of the growing season, spraying may occur. In all these cases, heavy equipment is traveling systematically through the field, modifying its surface and shifting some objects from one location to another. Surprisingly, in most cases the impact is relatively surficial.

Ignoring for a moment the practical considerations of barriers to excavation, the size of the research team or field school crew, the length of time available for the excavations, and the overall size of the area that needs to be sampled, it is important to keep in mind the primary focus of the research project. The primary interest is to gather information about the people who were using the site and why they were using it, from the standpoint of whatever issues are of top priority to the study. If a site is too large, the primary interest may be unclear. We do not want to spread the crew too thinly over the landscape, or place them so far apart that they cannot confer with the project director and share their findings with others in the group. Also, if the crew is an inexperienced one, they will need constant supervision to avoid loss of information they may not recognize. An added consideration will be the loss of

FIGURE 3-4
Excavation in areas where seeding and application of fertilizers has been scheduled by the landowner but not yet completed may cause delays.

FIGURE 3-5
*Excavation units opened to expose a wide horizontal area may
have soil columns (pilasters) left for stratigraphic control.*

time. If an excavation crew of inexperienced people is scattered over a large area, each member of the crew will have to wait for attention when questions arise. They may decide that their question is not important enough to delay the work, and they may continue to do what they are doing, without stopping to await the arrival of the crew leader or project director. What they are doing may not be the best approach in light of the discoveries—or questions—they have unearthed!

On the other hand, it is wise to space the crew members so that they do not get in one another's way when working. It may prove counterproductive if one person must stop while another is shoveling nearby, and also it can be dangerous! Shovels, trowels, artifact bags, labels, markers, tape measures, and sifters (*screens*) may become treacherous obstacles to those unaccustomed to their presence on the ground or beside excavations. Inexperienced excavators, and those moving from one area of the site to another, may neglect to place shovels with the blade edge down, for example. Although shovels and rakes have served as prime examples of accidents waiting to happen in many children's books on safety, it appears that these lessons need to be re-learned in the field! Not only are safety measures needed, but also those members who are new to a project may not be as meticulous about where these items are placed or how artifact containers are labeled, at first. Mix-ups may result from these situations and data may be lost.

FIGURE 3-6
*Shawnee-Minisink is an example of a large-scale excavation
with many people working in close proximity to one another.*

Even after practical considerations and primary interests have been taken into account, the question of where exactly to dig might remain. Rupee (1966), Hill (1970), Joukowsky (1981), and the "Photo Essay" and "Appendix A" of Turnbaugh, Jurmain, Nelson, and Kilgore's "The Archaeological Research Project" (1999, 493–501) provide an excellent array of site selection techniques and contexts or settings in which they work best. Others prefer the "educated guess approach" to a site. This technique often means picking a location *type* that, by experience at other sites, has proven productive, and selecting it for excavation. An example might be a slight rise in elevation in an otherwise flat floodplain of a river, the top of a ridge overlooking a river and freshwater spring, or the highest point of a small island. If artifacts are visible on the modern ground surface, this may suggest that more cultural materials may be present below the surface. Unfortunately, this may be misleading. Much depends on how the artifacts arrived at today's surface and what types of subsurface disturbances occur at the site.

SITE SURVEY AND SAMPLING

Once a site has been selected, the next step is conducting a site survey and doing sampling. Depending on the particular location, the number of people involved in the crew, and the time and money available for the project, there are a variety of approaches to *site survey*. First, we must differentiate between a site survey that refers to the comprehensive coverage of a large area such as a county or river basin, and the narrower, more intensive site survey of a particular location.

In the former case, all archival and library materials about the area are inventoried and plotted on a map. Usually, a U.S. Geological Survey Quadrangle Map is a good base map to use for this. If there are many sites to record, coding them by time period, size, cultural affiliation, and other criteria may be helpful. Sometimes a series of these maps is needed to show each type of *cultural component* (a particular set of artifactual materials for a specific time period) separately. Depending upon the topic of interest, roadways, townships, political units, fire districts, or educational boundaries may serve as divisions for concentrated study by members of the research crew.

In the latter case, where the intensive study of one location is the focus, creating a sampling design for study of one particular site may be the first step. How many test units are necessary to provide a representative view of what may be present in the site? What size should they be? What type of distribution of them will make the most of the time and personnel available? How will the test excavations be measured?

Depending on the measuring equipment available, the initial test excavation units may be measured in meters or feet. If you begin in one measurement system, a change later will make comparison and contrast of equivalent units more difficult, so try to select the system that will be used throughout the study. This is of major importance when several different sites may be studied at various times, for the purpose of eventual synthesis of all the information gathered from them, so try to plan ahead with this in mind.

A *grid system* will be created for the area involved in the study. This creates an artificial and arbitrary pattern of uniform-sized squares that cover the entire area of the study. The result looks like a giant piece of graph paper. Techniques for generating this arrangement for use in sampling will be presented in Chapter 5.

In any grid system, the sampling may be as exhaustive or as limited as time, personnel, and money dictate—or as the research design and questions require. Under cultural resource management contracts, there tend to be set percentages of test units required, and sometimes these samples seem inadequate. The results of the sampling may reflect quite clearly the adequacy or inadequacy of the sampling design by the degree to which archaeological questions are answered or remain unanswered.

When sampling is limited, concentration may be on one location where cultural materials—artifacts or human refuse—have been found on the surface. A smaller geographic area may be considered and the focus may be on mapping the limits and extent of a set of human materials and their context. Where the materials are scattered over the surface of a larger area, the whole region may be gridded, or the grid may be limited to the sampling of the specific area of the surface scatter. A large field might be gridded into 20-meter

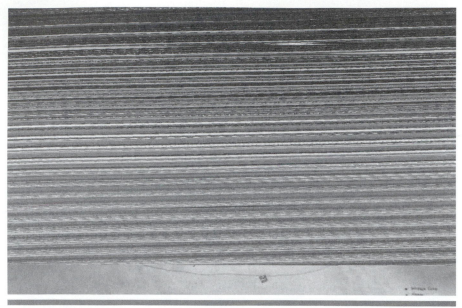

FIGURE 3-7
In some sites, areas are gridded for sampling; test excavations may sample several localities, as shown in this illustration of a central New York prehistoric site.

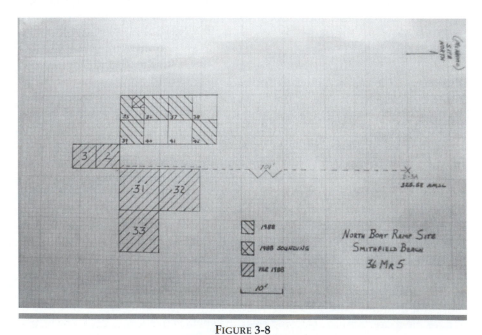

FIGURE 3-8
This is a graphed example of a contract project in which the archaeological sampling pattern was based on previous tests and planned modification of the project area.

squares, if the artifactual scatter is extensive, or in 10-meter squares, if these seem more manageable. The sampling might be limited to the plotting of each artifact on the surface *in situ* (in place), and the grid may serve only as a control and cross-check as measurements are taken and recorded.

Remember, the grid is an arbitrary, artificially-applied measuring device to help locate and show patterns of the distributed materials, and, later, to provide data for the artificial reconstruction of the site and its content and context in the laboratory analysis. These factors must be kept in perspective or amazing confusions of what is significant and why it matters may result. For instance, if the site has been disturbed by plowing or machine-rock-picking for many years, it is unlikely that mapping the exact location, to the tenth of a centimeter, of objects lying on the surface of the plowed field would be of value. However, if the site is a small, undisturbed rock shelter, the exact placement and orientation of each object (flat on one face of the flake, and angled in a particular direction where it might have been placed or might have fallen) might be significant and informative. Indeed, at the Shawnee-Minisink Site (36 MR 43) the exact location and orientation of a series of chert flakes from stone tool-making was plotted, and these data were correlated with the angle of slope of the soil stratum in which they occurred, about ten feet below today's ground surface. When researchers computer-graphed these artifacts, it became clear that they lay in a small streambed close to its bank (McNett 1985).

Figure 3-9 (on page 50) shows nails with strips of numbered masking tape attached to them. Each nail marked the location of a fragment of chert tool-making debris (*lithic debitage*) and charred matter plotted with the transit, and was recorded on a data sheet. These sheets were taken to the computer laboratory where a keypunch technician entered all the data into the computer for plotting. This particular set of plotted artifacts was located at ten feet below today's ground surface, adjacent to the massive beams (referred to as "dead men") supporting the shoring used to protect the excavators. At the same depth, and less than two feet away, the sole projectile point (referred to as a "Clovis-style" projectile point) was found.

Although the research goal and hypotheses to be tested are of importance when devising an appropriate sampling design, as are the types of materials and the sites involved in the project, another consideration may be the likelihood of the site's imminent destruction through other means. Not all archaeology hinges on, or should be geared to, the demolition of a site or its environmental context by construction or land-leveling activity. However, if there are two similar sites, one endangered by construction and the other apparently safe for the present, the former should receive attention first, and perhaps with a greater degree of emphasis and sampling coverage, if no alternative means of preserving it can be found.

If a site is to be excavated on a large scale (many acres or hectares or neighborhoods in a town, for example), another consideration arises. Anthropological archaeology of today includes a vast array of techniques for gathering

FIGURE 3-9
Chert flakes were marked for mapping at Shawnee-Minisink Site, Pennsylvania.

information about earlier residents of a location, their environment, their tools, foods, housing, fire-making and using techniques and preferences, their clothing, their exploitation of local resources, and numerous other kinds of knowledge. Some of these techniques are only a few years old in archaeological usage. Others are extremely costly and may not be available for many research projects. What might be added to current methods and skills of recovery in ten, twenty, or one hundred years? Currently, wherever possible, sections of sites are left unexcavated, *by choice*, to provide the option for future archaeologists with new skills and insights (and different research questions) to expand our data bank of information about specific cultural groups, behaviors, and environmental adaptions or pressures.

Returning to the purpose of this chapter, how *do* we know where to dig? We have described two levels of survey—one that explores a multi-acre area to locate segments that should be examined subsurficially, and the second that focuses on spots where particular kinds of artifactual materials occur on the surface or where they are concentrated most densely. These indications may dictate where excavation will occur. One hypothesis for testing would be that subsurface materials are a continuation of surface materials. Its corollary would be, if subsurface materials are not a continuation of materials found on the surface, why and how do they differ, and what do these differences imply?

The most important consideration of all is what sort of information the archaeologist seeks. Why is the search focused on this particular area (the rationale for the entire research project), and what specific data, when they are found, are to be emphasized? At the same time, every effort will be made by the archaeologist to gather as much information about the site and its locality as possible, whether this fits the particular focus of attention or is peripheral to it. This is the ideal. Often the reality falls far short of this aim.

RESEARCH DESIGN

Why do we do archaeology? What does the archaeologist want to know about the people and the place? Are there questions about the location, size, and distribution of settlements created by a particular group of people? Are there suggestions that the influx of a new group of people may have caused the earlier residents to leave? Were there changes in climate or available resources that led to changes in settlement and subsistence patterns for a particular group? The archaeologist's approach to the area or the site will reflect the research questions. The questions should help pinpoint sets of sites with the appropriate artifactual remains visible or previously recorded for them. Based on these data, a sampling design for excavation may be developed to fit. The survey may be a *stratified* one where topographic features, such as streambeds or stream shores, distinctive rock outcroppings, swamps, or other characteristics of the landscape are included as part of the sample—rather than relying on a strict random selection from the whole geographic area. Even with this type of excavation choice, a random sample of units within each *stratum* or *topographic zone* of the overall grid may be chosen. Sometimes a formula will be devised to include each topographic locality in proportion to its frequency or land area within a particular region. This may be dependent upon the archaeologist's previous understanding of exploitation patterns of groups similar to the one being studied, or it may be based upon strict geographic areal units.

If the purpose of the research is to determine trade networks for particular raw materials or finished products, the suspected trade route area and any "logical" alternates might get more concentrated attention, along with the source areas for the raw materials, the areas at greatest distance from those in which the item or material has been found, and then other locations that are considered likely to contribute pertinent information from the largest range of locations. Perhaps there will be consideration of what was traded for the raw materials and finished products, who the traders or intermediaries might have been and what their "cut," payment, or recompense might have been. Maximum dispersal of sampling units, rather than a more concentrated effort in a few areas, might be the best strategy. This often expands the distribution of known locations with direct connection to the research question, and may reveal otherwise unexpected and unknown factors that have influenced the trade system.

Unfortunately, all of this logic may be invalid because it is the logic of an archaeologist of today, not that of the maker and user of the resources or those utilizing the trade network. Therefore, it is essential to try to imagine other ways of thinking about trade that might differ from our current perceptions. To do this, archaeologists study other groups of people, especially modern ones known through ethnographic studies as well as earlier ones known from archaeological research in different regions. Ideally, there would be living descendants who might provide an oral history of how their ancestors carried out trade. This often provides some of the best angles to consider as the research is planned.

An example of other ways of thinking was found many years ago by anthropologist Bronislaw Malinowski. In his study of the Trobriand Islanders, he discovered that trade, for what we might call ritual reasons, included exchange of items the trade partners passed back and forth to reinforce ties between them. The items traded were available in both locations without trade being "needed." The function of this procedure had nothing to do with our notions of exchanging one item of value for something we need to get from somewhere else (Malinowski 1922).

SOME SURFACE COLLECTION TECHNIQUES

The purpose of a collection of artifactual material from the surface of an archaeological site is to gain new information about the site, its context, and the people who created and used the site. You want to learn as much as possible about who the people may have been, what they were doing there, where they came from, where they might have gone next, and why and how long they stayed in this site. Merely picking up artifacts from a site because you recognize that they are artifacts is not the best approach. Once the objects have been moved, by you or by anyone else, the "event" of their arrival in that location has been erased. You have tampered with the evidence, changed the picture of the past. You may argue that the objects are on the surface and have been disturbed previously. This is probable, but how and why were they moved, when were they moved, and where were they before they were moved? Careful inspection of the artifacts and their contexts, both in a very narrow sense and in a broader study of their associations with other artifacts and environmental factors, may show answers to questions that will be unanswerable otherwise.

The point is that tampering with the evidence without careful consideration of the context and relationships of one item to the others is destructive, and that merely gathering up objects provides much less information than it contributes. Thus, *uncontrolled collection*, as this is called, is characterized by picking up any or all types of artifactual material from one or many areas. This is discouraged by most archaeologists. Usually, with uncontrolled collection, not every artifact that is present is being collected either. Thus, the variety, type, and quantities of materials present in the site will be biased by this type of "sampling."

Controlled collections, on the other hand, may be carried out in a number of ways to provide useful archaeological information about settlement pattern, lithic or ceramic preferences of the site users, activity area usage, so-called "toss and throw zones," or for other cultural information. The time, money, purpose of the study, and likelihood that the materials will be lost if they are not removed, may be factors to consider. Here are some of the ways in which such a collection might be carried out so that a maximum amount of information is retrieved. In all cases, a fairly detailed map of the location and its context is essential so that the collection units and their content are keyed to it.

1. Gather all recognizable "tools" from a specified (and mapped!) area or "tools and recognizable artifactual debris" from a specified (and mapped!) area.

2. Lay out a grid of the area to be collected (like a piece of graph paper, only much larger!) and collect each block or square, or other type of unit shape, within the grid, separately, and bag the materials collected, by block or square, or whatever unit shape you have selected, in labeled bags. Possibly, "tools and recognizable artifactual debris" might be the materials collected.

3. Conduct sampling within a controlled collection. Either collect, as in "2," everything artifactual from every third square or block (or fifth, or tenth ...), placing the materials collected in separate, labeled bags or, use a *random number table* to determine which squares or blocks to collect, and carry out the same process.

4. Conduct stratified sampling within a controlled collection. Collect a specified number of squares or blocks (randomly) from each topographically different area within the site, and carry out the same process as in "3." In this system, you might collect five blocks in a row from each of a series of environmental settings, for example, the beach, the upper terrace, the mountain ridge, the rock quarry, and so forth.

5. *Plot in* (map the exact locations) and collect all tools and other cultural debris, from a particular sampling unit. Bag the materials in labeled bags for each separate unit, with identifiers for each of the objects plotted. Units chosen for sampling may be arbitrary ones or might be based upon one of the sampling strategies mentioned earlier. A unit, square, or block might be an approximation of the location of each artifact, with distance and angles plotted from the *master datum point* (point from which all measurements within the site are made, and for which there are several other reference points for relocation of the datum if it is destroyed in the future).

6. Use the dog leash method. Gather all artifacts and artifactual debris within your reach (*radius*) when you are attached to a leash or string affixed to a given point. Bag materials collected in labeled bags for the circle for which the leash provides the radius.

Caution: The purpose of any of these sampling techniques is to determine the size, nature, and general cultural content of the site, on the basis of surficial materials. Usually, the sampling is just a preliminary step in an elaborate strategy to test the site more extensively, and to determine the degree of *cultural integrity* (lack of disturbance of materials) of the site and their current locational contexts on the surface. Frequently, material found on the surface indicates that there are other materials buried somewhere nearby, but this is not always the case. The reasons for this must be determined through additional study of surface and subsurface information, and the context of the site itself.

SUBSURFACE SAMPLING

Some of the same strategies may be used for subsurface sampling that have been listed for surface study. However, in most cases, when excavation occurs, all artifacts and artifactual debris is plotted, collected and recorded, in its specific context. Some sampling may be based on the random number table, selection of every fifth, tenth, or some other number of squares in a gridded site, or with allowance for sampling of diverse topographic areas (*stratified sampling*). Why would it be useful to consider different elevations? Think about where you do specific things: If you are skipping stones, fishing, digging clams, or gathering plants that are found near water, those activities should be reflected by appropriate "debris" from them; if you are collecting nuts, hunting plants or animals that inhabit hilltops, that is where you would leave behind clues to those actions. If flooding is likely, perhaps your camp, house, storage facility, and many other structures would be placed where this would not be a problem. Naturally, this is today's logic based upon some general types of reasons. Certainly, there could be cases in which even sites that flood frequently could have been the favored ones, at least between floods! The point is that you want to try to imagine, using the best logic available, what types of factors might result in people using one or another of the diverse locations within an area. To avoid emphasizing your own preconceived notions too much, selections of random samples in the diverse localities may be of some help.

SUMMARY

Knowing where to dig is not a foregone conclusion! On some occasions, there are burned and discolored areas that represent old, frequently reused fireplaces, which yield extensive evidence of what was burned, what was cooked, and what was discarded. In some parts of the world, there are visible ruins of ancient towns, walls, stone fences, or other structures that delineate the major portions of a site. Elsewhere, there may be changes in vegetation, frequently, visible only at some seasons of the year, or from the air, which outline sub-surface buried walls and other large-scale rubble.

However, surface indications are often misleading and subsurface materials display little resemblance to them. Sometimes virtually all surface indications have been obliterated by plowing, jungle growth, rock-picking (by hand and machine in some regions), gravel-quarrying, or other means. Sometimes surface indications were never extensive enough to survive gradual decay and natural disintegration. Examples of fragile sites like these are spots where someone stopped to gather a few medicinal plants, burned a tiny bit of sacred tobacco, or left a few feathers or sticks to mark their passage.

Sometimes subsurface features are discovered by a combination of surface survey and core-boring or auguring. Where one bores or augers and how the information is understood and recorded will depend on the project, the type of equipment, the skill of the workers and their director, and the nature of the soils themselves.

For example, flood plains tend to have deep layers of accumulated *alluvium* (flood-deposited silt). Here, the boring activity needs to be deep enough to provide for many years of accumulation in the sample. Only in this way will the boring reflect the time that has elapsed since the site usage by the group of interest to the researcher. However, one flood can deposit several inches, or several feet, of alluvium! Another flood in the same location at another time may add to this or scour off several inches or several feet of the silt!

On a hillside, soils may be very thin and may be underlain by solid bedrock. Here, coring or auguring will be pointless except to prove that bedrock is a scant few inches below the current surface. In some places on the hillside, there will be no layer of soil at all, merely exposed rock. Elsewhere, there may be pockets of somewhat deeper soil deposits. In each case, though, records should show what was done, or not done, and what was observed. Negative evidence can be important as an indication that the researcher looked in all the places.

In any location, especially in areas of extensive, recent glaciation, the quantity of rock may make auguring with manual equipment virtually impossible and unproductive. Elsewhere, anything that turns out to be solid or rocklike may indicate an archaeologically relevant hidden feature. This latter situation would make the auguring method far more useful and would make it an automatic tool for probing research in those localities. An example of this might be sandy beach areas where rocks are absent, except when carried in by people.

Thus, every bit of research, every question asked, every step in the project, will reflect the biases of the research design and the orientation of the researcher (often referred to as our "cultural blinders"). A narrow focus may result in loss of important cultural information. How one knows where to dig is both luck and educated guessing. How to select the best sampling approach for a particular area or site will depend on the area and the questions asked. How much is to be excavated depends on the scope of the project and its related site or sites. Other determinants are the practical considerations of time, personnel, money, and permissions or permits to carry out the work in a particular place. Finally, leaving a portion of the site for future studies using newer and better research tools should be planned, whenever it is feasible.

Exercise   Draw a diagram in which you show furniture arranged in a room (rough squares, rectangles, circles, and so forth to represent them will do). Make this "room arrangement" fit a scale of about a 6-inch by 6-inch square. Next, using the same-sized square for your borders, diagram a segment of a yard in which there is a tree, three plants (tomato or whatever), a pathway, and a birdbath.

Finally, again, using the same-sized square for your borders, diagram a segment of a campsite in which there is a barbecue pit, tent, woodpile, set of markers showing where your campsite ends and the next one begins, trash can, and water pump.

Now, place these three diagrams one on top of the other and hold them up to the light. Are there open spaces where none of them have any "cultural materials" in them? Are there places where all of the "features or artifacts" occur one on top of the other?

Here comes the most telling step in the exercise! Draw a 6-inch x 6-inch square with horizontal and vertical lines within it at 1/2-inch intervals. Very lightly, check off any six of these squares, and then, place this grid on top of each of your other three diagrams to see what you did or did not "get" when you checked the six squares. Erase the six squares and select any six alternate ones (or use a random number table to select the ones to use) and see how you do. Which of the "features" in each of your diagrams did you miss and which did you find? This is an extremely simple (and somewhat ideal) example of site sampling. First, you know there are features present in the area you are sampling; second, when you drew the diagrams, probably you tended to "center" things the way we are taught to do in art classes and decorating projects; third, the universe is quite small, so that your choices rarely miss everything!

HOW DO WE BEGIN?

BEARING IN MIND THAT EVERY ARCHAEOLOGICAL SITE IS UNIQUE AND REQUIRES modifications of techniques to fit the situation, a first step will be for the director and field crew to study the area in which a site is located. Using a U.S. Geological Survey map, often a 7.5 foot quadrangle map, the researchers will check the site's general position in space, its geographic context, its contours, and its neighboring landmarks—that is, what is on and around the location. When they are available, it is useful to look at the Sanborn Fire Insurance maps devised in many populated areas within the past century or so, to see what historic structures were plotted on them. Atlases, especially historic atlases of various communities, often show old roadways, millraces, ponds, houses, sheds, tanneries, shops, and other landmarks that may or may not be apparent from later maps. Today, there are a number of excellent tools to expand on basic topographic maps, maps from a local historical society, or those from the local Chamber of Commerce. An example of an informative and easily navigated Web address is the Encarta Learning Zone TerraServer at <http://terraserver.microsoft.com/image.asp>. It includes aerial photographs and options that enable the researcher to inspect a location closely and to retrieve its map coordinates. Although there are a number of CD-ROM software mapping programs available, including Rand McNally's "TripMaker™" and DeLorme's "Map'N'Go™," the Internet offerings continue to provide more and more options if the student explores the updated possibilities.

Next, a trip to the site location enables the researchers to compare the maps to the real world. Depending on the situation, the step prior to site entry may be a meeting with the landowners to get permission, preferably in writing, to go on the property or to make an archaeological study of it.

Usually, this step has occurred before the field school students enter the picture. However, it is wise and often more diplomatic to introduce the crew to the landowners. In the case of state or federal property, it is important to make contact with the local representatives of the agency involved, and to include the student researchers in this process, too. This is essential for possible problems or emergencies. Also, it is helpful to acquaint those working on a project with those whose cooperation is vital to the success of the project. In some countries, there are often regulations as to who works where and under what sort of permit and local supervision. These regulations may alter many of the questions asked, determine whether an interpreter will be needed, and perhaps present other problems specific to those locations.

During these preliminaries, the landowner will be asked about any objects that have been found on the property and any features of the landscape that might be of interest and importance. What is asked and how it is asked depends on the landowner's understanding of what you want, as well as the type of site location you hope to study. In one case, you may be looking for Native American tools, refuse dumps, house sites, fishing camps, or meeting places. However, animal bones, colonial china, metal objects, brick, and other historic debris may tell of other uses made of the lands. In other cases, you may be concerned about old fence lines or roads, Roman coins, glazed ceramics, or other kinds of evidence of sites in European areas. Sometimes, a researcher's questions and interest will spark a memory of previous site usage or discoveries that the landowner had forgotten or considered insignificant. Often, there need to be several interviews or visits with the landowners as the project gets under way. Again, each visit may elicit new information and new questions from you. Keep in mind, however, that the landowner may not have time or interest in too much quizzing from you. This should be handled with patience and consideration, as well as diplomacy.

Once the fundamental contacts and arrangements have been formalized (agreements may include whether researchers will pay for crop damage, replant destroyed sod, walk rather than drive heavy vehicles onto the property, and so forth), the actual field work can begin. Quite often the arrangements, which initially seemed firm, will need to be reworked as the property owner sees the actual field equipment and personnel in action. This appears to be the case no matter how much preplanning has been done. It should not be viewed as a point against the project director, nor against the landowner. Probably it could not have been averted by some additional earlier action. Frequently, when a landowner realizes that "digging" will occur, he or she may envision, and object to, a major stripping of a large section of the property. While this may be the process in some cases, often the excavations are much smaller in scale than the landowner envisioned. Usually, the work is organized carefully, with efforts to localize soils that are excavated and screened, so that they can be replaced in the holes created once the work is completed. Once the landowner is assured that topsoil will be backfilled on top of the subsoils, the sod will be replaced once the work is done, and no deep holes will be left unprotected, his or her concerns are usually allayed.

Work in a cornfield, for example, may require some scheduling around the farmer's activities. If plowing or discing have occurred, but planting has not, perhaps archaeologists can walk the field, but should not begin any placement of equipment in the field until the planting is completed. Once planting is finished, the young seedlings are up, and good weather develops, Agway or some other supplier of fertilizers and other chemicals may be scheduled to spray the field—sometime. Experience proves that, although the sprayers may say it does not matter, it is wise to leave the field when the truck arrives and stay away until the chemicals have dispersed. Some farmers may later return to the fields, at intervals, to cultivate or weed a crop. The machinery for this can demolish archaeological equipment, and some of the archaeological equipment can damage the farmer's machinery (wire flagging used to mark locations in the field, for example, can become tangled in farm equipment).

Farmers who have worked with archaeologists previously may be aware of these factors, but many are not. Therefore, it is to our advantage to note possible hazards and conflicts and try to discuss them in advance, when possible. Sometimes a student will be aware of dangers or potential problems unknown to the director. Most researchers welcome this information, so do not hesitate to share it!

After all the delays—perhaps with false-starts—it is time to go onto the site. First, the director and crew walk over the land scrutinizing the terrain, vegetation, and all open ground surfaces for any clues to human land use, besides the current farming activity. Sometimes students cannot distinguish between modern and "old" objects. Do not be discouraged if an object that excited you turns out to be a fragment of modern drainage tile! At least you noted the object and did not overlook it! Also, only through asking and making some mistakes, do we learn about what we find. Generally items such as "modern" metal, glass, newspaper, plastic, and fertilizer pellets are ignored, except for recording them in the field notebooks as "surface debris present," and learning to identify and distinguish them from other items. Any "older" materials or surface features are noted carefully, and may be marked with wooden or metal flags for future reference. Usually, it is helpful to keep a notebook in which every item or cluster of items, every plowed area, every ditch, every vehicle turn-around area, every clump of trees, every separate feature— modern/artificial or natural—is recorded. The reason we do this is to provide as much of a record of the more recent activities at the site as possible, thereby preventing, if possible, misinterpretation of these features after excavation is under way and some of them have been obliterated. Throughout this process, it is useful to confer with the landowner to determine what holes have been dug for drainage, where rubble or manure have been dumped or buried, and similar kinds of information.

Any time something unusual is located, it is helpful and exciting to let the landowner know! Sometimes, such things trigger a memory of other types of information that may be relayed to the archaeologists. As an example, in the summer of 1997 the field school crew located a badly corroded adjustable wrench in the field. It was cleaned up and returned to the landowner, who related the story of the occasion when it was lost! During that conversation, he mentioned that until he began farming twenty-five years ago, the field had been a hay field as far back as there had been people living in the area. This helped us understand how portions of the field had been protected from erosion and from deep plowing prior to the current shallow-tilling practices. Learning why soil disturbances were more shallow than anticipated provided hope that post-mold patterns from structures or storage pits would remain intact below the plowed stratum.

To conclude, there are unexpected events in every archaeological experience. Some prove to be alarming, like close encounters with fertilizers and weed sprayers. Others may be exciting contributions to knowledge.

THE EXCAVATIONS: HOW DO
WE DIG ARCHAEOLOGICALLY?

A T LAST, IT IS TIME FOR EXCAVATION! ALL THE PRELIMINARY RESEARCH AND tantalizing walk-overs have occurred. Some areas have been marked with flagging because something unusual was found on the surface.

Everyone has been issued a set of equipment and probably a kit in which to store the tools. Each person is responsible for the kit and its contents. The kits are carried out into the research area and placed close to the portion of the site where the researchers anticipate working. What is in the kit? What are all the other tools of the trade? Why are these used and others are not?

TOOLS OF THE TRADE

Basic archaeological equipment consists of shovels, both pointed and flat-bladed, screens or sifters, ranging in size from those the size of a trash can lid to huge 10-foot square standing-rocker or sliding screens. The mesh through which soils will be sifted ranges from 1/2 inch to 1/16 inch. Sometimes, there are layers of different mesh size with the largest gauge on top, to the small-est gauge on the bottom, to sort materials right down to the tiniest fragments. Other equipment includes buckets of various sizes; wheelbarrows (some-times); wooden or metal stakes; a file to sharpen metal tools; hammers or mauls to hammer the stakes; nails, screwdrivers, screws and wing nuts to replace those that might get lost from the screens; *transit* or Level-All (sur-veying instruments); compass; *plumb bob* (pointed weight suspended from a string for use in measuring depths below a particular elevation) and string; plane table or other mapping surface; *stadia rod* (stiff extension ruler often 20 feet tall when opened); camera equipment and film; 100-foot or 100-meter tapes; nonstretch string; flagging; first-aid kit; sterile gloves (for avoiding infections and for retrieving artifactual materials without contaminating them); aluminum foil, assorted paper, plastic, and metal containers for samples; plastic scoops or dust pans; rolls of heavy plastic sheeting; loose-leaf notebooks and record sheets, and miscellaneous permanent magic markers, pens, pencils, erasers, rulers, and pencil-sharpeners; masking tape; duct tape for repairs; Munsell Soil Color Charts, PH and Moisture Meters for soil testing; and computer equipment, if available. Waterless hand-cleaner, Handi-wipes™, and toilet paper are important for sanitary purposes. Probably, today, a cell phone would be standard equipment in most areas, too. Many of these items are needed in addition to the student tool kits.

The student kits include masons' trowels; paint brushes; dental picks; metal tape measures, preferably with graduated inches and centimeters on them; whisk brooms; a line level and piece of string about 10-feet long; permanent magic markers for labeling; pens, pencils, small ruler and protractor; and field notebooks (we use a water-resistant hip-pocket-sized, cloth-bound, sewn book with lined sheets on the left and graph paper on the right side of each page). Pencil sharpeners and magnifying glasses, as well as erasers and pocket knives, are useful additions to the kit.

For the laboratory, many of the same items are needed, but to these are added buckets and smaller containers for washing artifacts; masses of newspaper for drying tables, unless there are screened drying racks; labeling equipment (pens with many nibs, India ink, white and clear butyrate dope for pre- and post-labeling of artifacts, unless another system is in use with stamping devices); soil sampling kits and chemicals; Moh hardness testers; and many sizes, shapes, and varieties of acid-free storage containers. Binocular microscopes, special lighting for inspection of materials and photographing them, a drawing table, light table, other photographic equipment, film, and a darkroom may be part of the facilities. Today, digital cameras and videotaping equipment often provide options for more immediate, less time-consuming retrieval and recording of information.

Of course, many archaeological facilities do not have the full complement of photographic equipment and rely on other offices for these. The same may be the case for *spectrographic microscopes* (these instruments are used to identify elements contained in lithic samples, including clay pottery; the distinctive wavelengths or colors can be measured by specialists so that the content and natural source of the sample can be located), as well as equipment and personnel for geological, floral, and faunal analysis, and some aspects of the computerization processes. For instance, computerized mapping and scanning may be done through one office, rather than in individualized ones. Ideally, though, the student should receive at least elementary training in the techniques these employ. This training is important because it demonstrates why accuracy and thoroughness in the field and laboratory are essential. Often, there appear to be meaningless categories of information with codes that are an annoyance to the field researcher. However, if there has been some instruction in advance that demonstrates how these data are to be used, it is easier to confirm in the field. Each mistake in the field or laboratory means greater problems when the data are computerized, possibly resulting in insurmountable problems and lost data!

This array of field and laboratory equipment is augmented by odds and ends of specialized tools that particular archaeologists prefer or specific projects need. On the first few days of field work, students may be overwhelmed and discouraged by all the "necessities." Must all of these be used right away by every student? Must everything be carried out into the field each day, and back at the end of the day? How can all the necessary warnings about what to do and what not to do be communicated? The sensation is much like being thrown into an airplane cockpit with all its gadgetry and being told to fly the plane. The procedure for initiating new students to field work is the same. But, eventually, one learns a "drill." The work is organized with a checklist of things to remember, items to take, jobs to be done, and a particular order for these, as well as specific techniques for doing these.

Needless to say, since the work is governed, in part, by what is encountered, the "drill" will vary to fit what is found. However, at every archaeological site, the major goal is the same: to recover every bit of information that one can because once the site is excavated, the site is destroyed. There are no second chances. Sloppy work at any stage will result in lost or inaccurate information. This is true especially when one is mapping the site and plotting objects that have been found *in situ*, and locating them on a scale map of the site or units within it. The general records of what is found in various blocks or units, and under what conditions they have been found, are of equal significance. Do not assume that you or someone else will remember the details that are left out of the records!

DIG?

Suddenly, the tripod, stadia rod, and transit, or Level-All, are handed to members of the crew, a compass is given to another person, and a maul, ball of string, and a batch of pointed stakes are given to other members of the crew. Don't tell me we aren't going to start digging after all this anticipation and carting of equipment from vehicles to the staging area in the site! No, first, the site must be *gridded*. What this means is that the entire area of study, or at least the segment to be emphasized right away, must be measured out in equal units, all of which can be reckoned from one or more points that will now be determined. Although there are numerous kinds of survey equipment, from the simplest compass to the most sophisticated *Total Station* (a Total Station is an instrument for mapping or surveying a site; it consists of the powered transit-like mechanism on a tripod and a rod with a prism; the rod is taken to the location to be recorded and the Total Station survey instrument shoots an infrared beam to the prism; the beam, in turn, is registered on the dials of the survey instrument indicating distance to the prism, slope, and relation to true and magnetic north; sometimes computers are attached to record these data) or laser transit with connections to computers and international mapping coordinators, the basic purpose and at least some of the procedures are the same.

PROCEDURES FOR CREATING A SITE GRID

The first step is to select, arbitrarily, a convenient point on the site to set up a surveying instrument. If possible and if practical, select a spot that can remain undisturbed and stable (and "permanent," if feasible) throughout the project. To make it permanent, install a long (2–3-feet long) metal rod (1/2 inch construction *rebar*—reinforcement rod—is usually adequate). This point will be known as *datum*, or the *0-0 point*, for the site. From it, all other reference points will be measured.

Over this arbitrary point (datum), set up the surveying instrument being sure that it is *plumb* (leveling it with the mechanisms on it, and suspending a plumb bob on a string from the hook beneath the surveying instrument). The pointed base of the plumb bob will be centered exactly over the rebar marking datum.

For future reference, the master datum point should be *tied in* (located in space through its exact location in relationship to several other points) with two or three other "permanent" points within relatively easy view. This can be done by sighting three different objects (telephone poles, monuments, specific corners of houses, U.S. Geological Survey Benchmarks) and recording their angles (degrees east or west of north, and distances from the master datum). The importance of this procedure cannot be overemphasized. Even a rebar may be demolished if there is future destruction of that area of the site. The reference could be relocated if the other reference points remained, however. Do not rely on a "lone tree in field" or even a fence line for reference points because the tree may be struck by lightning, plowed out, or cut for firewood, eradicating the reference point. Worst still, is the "lone tree" that becomes part of an assortment of scattered "lone trees," that, by chance, have grown rapidly to similar size! Highway survey markers are fairly helpful, as are bridge abutments, although they, too, may move or disappear over time. In one site, we used a U.S. Geological Survey Benchmark located beside an abandoned railroad trestle, only to return a few years later to discover the trestle and marker had been bulldozed away. As you can see, the more permanent points of reference you locate and document to help you establish the site grid, the better the chances are that at least one of them will be there in the future!

Ideally, the exact elevation above mean sea level of the master datum will be established before excavation begins. This is accomplished by contacting the U.S. Geological Survey to determine the elevation above mean sea level of the benchmark utilized for reference at the site. Each of these metal-on-concrete markers has a number designation from which the elevation can be ascertained. The next step is to calculate the difference in elevation between the benchmark and the site datum point. To achieve this, measure the height of the surveying instrument by standing the stadia rod directly in front of it (be sure the survey instrument is level and the stadia rod is perpendicular to the ground). This height is referred to as *instrument height*, or IH. Next, have the rod person place the stadia rod perpendicular to the top of the benchmark (usually its top is at ground surface) and measure the elevation above the ground surface at the benchmark, in relation to the elevation of the surveying instrument. Once the elevation of the benchmark above mean sea level has been learned, one subtracts the IH of the survey instrument from the height of the stadia rod at the benchmark to determine the elevation of the master datum point.

Using a magnetic compass, sight a northern line from the datum to the northern end of the site, and at the same time, set the surveying instrument with this compass to register north. Two crew members will be sent to that (north) location, one holding the stadia rod upright and plumb (that is, perpendicular to the ground) at that north location. The second person, using the maul and a wooden stake, will hammer the stake into the ground to mark that location. To prevent potential confusion at a later date, correction should be made for *true north*. A magnetic compass has a magnetic needle that pivots freely. Its needle aligns itself with the earth's magnetic field so that one end of the needle points to magnetic north. The north magnetic pole is in northern Canada. A magnetic compass needle pivots to one of the two points near opposite ends of a magnet, toward which the earth's magnetic lines of force are oriented and concentrated. If the magnet is permitted to rotate in all directions by use of a central pivot, one pointer will point in the direction of the earth's magnetic pole near the North Pole, or "north-seeking" or positive pole of the magnet; the other pole is the "south-seeking" or negative pole (*Dictionary of Geological Terms*, revised edition 1976, American Geological Institute, Doubleday Anchor Publication, pp. 265–266).

The face of a magnetic compass has a circle marked or graduated in quadrants (quarters) from 0 degrees to 90 degrees, both east and west and from both the north and south points of the compass. The magnetized steel needle is supported on a steel pivot and jeweled bearing and counterbalanced against the dip of the needle. An arrow marking north-south serves as the fixed line of sight. The needle dips down to the north, so the counterbalance is placed south of the pivot and serves to indicate the north and south ends of the needle. Note that the graduated circle turns while the needle remains stationary on its pivot, so that the west and east points of the circle are interchanged, to give the correct bearing if the north end of the needle is read. (These procedures have been tested by numerous classes of college students around New York State who have been trained by avocational archaeologists Barbara and Gordon De Angelo. They volunteer their time, and the use of their Total Station, to provide survey workshops to archaeology students.)

Next, rotate the surveying instrument 180 degrees from the true north setting established with the compass (be sure to recheck that it is level once it is rotated) and sight to the southern end of the site. With maul and stake, hammer in a stake at the south end of the site. Recheck the initial sighting by rotating the surveying instrument 180 degrees (check level) back to the initial position and check the position of the northernmost stake. The north-south line is established. This line can be extended in either direction if at a later date the site is found to extend beyond what were thought to be its boundaries. Often, the north-south baseline is established in a manner that will enable the designation of all the excavation units within the gridded site to lie either completely east of the line or completely west of the line (ideally). The reason this is done is to avoid one source of error in the labeling process. Depending upon the equipment used, the procedure for site layout varies.

Now, rotate the surveying instrument 90 degrees (check the level) to east or west, and hammer in another stake at the outer boundary of the site. Rotate the surveying instrument 180 degrees (check level) to complete the east-west line, and hammer in a stake at that outer boundary. Why is such a production made about the leveling of the surveying instrument? Because if this is not done, measurements may be off by a noticeable amount and the grid will be uneven.

FIGURE 5-1
Set up and level the Level-All at 0-0 point.

If a Total Station were used for these procedures, the computerized instrument would provide distance, slope distance, and angles. Thus, it would be possible to utilize this instrument to measure locations of all stakes at intervals along the north-south line. However, many researchers do not have access to this equipment. Further, in my view, it is to the student's advantage to understand what the measurements are and how they are generated. Then, when the more expensive and sophisticated equipment is available, moments of malfunction may be evident to the experienced researcher. Without previous experience achieving these measurements, it is more difficult to recognize problems when only the computerized system is utilized.

From the north-south and east-west lines, a grid of any size that is practical for excavation or surface survey work can be established (i.e., 5 feet, 10 feet, 1 meter, 3 meters) by measuring along the north-south or east-west line and installing stakes at the selected distances from datum. After one side of a square or excavation unit has been established, the remainder of the square can be created by using *triangulation*.

TRIANGULATION

The site is measured out and staked at equal intervals. This will create squares, all of equal size. Each of these squares will be given a distinctive label that identifies it. Why do we do this? The purpose of sampling is to set up controls, that is, to arrange areas that will be tested so that their exact location—horizontal and vertical—can be diagrammed. By establishing a grid that covers the area from which your sample will come, you will be able to relocate each unit, based on its unique label, within the grid for sampling and for plotting on graph paper. This way, there will be a written replica of where work was done and where each object found within the grid was encountered. Since you plan to alter the appearance of the sampled area, this will serve as a record to help you reconstruct what was done and exactly where it was done.

Once your *baseline* (north-south/east-west) is established, recorded, and tied to other points, it is time to measure along its length, placing stakes in the ground at regular intervals. From this line (using the surveying equipment if it provides distances, angles, and elevations), sets of squares are measured, creating a grid (see diagram on page 69). Squares, or units, within the grid are chosen (at random, at selected intervals, or in clusters) for sampling (excavation).

If it is not possible to set up a grid with a Total Station, three people with two tape measures can triangulate squares from the baseline. Since the squares are set up at a right angle from the baseline, there is a simple procedure for this process. We shall use a 1-meter by 1-meter square as an example. If each side of the square is 1 meter, and the potential sides are *a*, *b*, *c*, and *d*, the formula would be the square root of *a* times *a*, plus *b* times *b*, equals the hypotenuse, or diagonal, of the square (*a*, *b*, *c*, *d*). The same procedure applies for any sized square, as long as the *hypotenuse* (side of the right triangle across from the right angle—the diagonal of a square) is calculated accurately. The diagonal, or hypotenuse, of a 1-meter square is 1.414 meters. (This is based upon the Pythagorean Theorem: In a right-triangle, the square root of the sum of the squares of the two adjacent sides equals the diagonal or hypotenuse.)

Here is the procedure for triangulation: Person A stands at one of the two measured marker stakes along the baseline, holding one end of the tape measure. Person B stands at the second of the two measured marker stakes along the baseline, holding one end of a second tape measure. Person C extends the other end of Person A's tape measure to 1.414 meters (realistically, to about 1.4 meters) and Person B's tape measure to 1 meter. Now, comes the hard part! Person C has two ends of tape measures in hand, and must move them from side to side until the two points on the tapes meet exactly. If there is an available Person D, that person can hammer in a stake right at the spot where the two tape measures cross. This *should* provide the third side of the 1-meter by 1-meter square. Reversing the two tapes, so that Person A holds the tape at 1.414 meters and Person B holds the tape at 1 meter, Person C will repeat the process for the fourth corner of the 1-meter square. The moment of reckoning comes when the three sides of the square are measured, stake-to-stake, to see whether each side is 1 meter in each direction! If not, the triangulation process should be repeated until the measurements are corrected. If this is not done, any additional units or squares measured from this one will be skewed. Also, if the "square" is not "square" it will become much more noticeable after excavation has begun! Accuracy is extremely important for record-keeping and for eventual opening of sets of units along the north-south or east-west lines to expose a linear strip of stratigraphy! Irregularities in soils and the action of rain, drying, or rodent activities during excavation create enough control problems without adding human errors to them.

Labels for the squares within the grid may be tagged in many different ways, but a standard one begins at the master datum point (0-0), the point of reference from which all other points may be calculated. This first square or unit is labeled N0 E0 (or, if the excavation unit lies west of the baseline, N0 W5). "N" refers to north; "E," "W," or "S" would refer to east, west, or south, respectively. Usually, by convention (and in an effort to make it possible for any other archaeologist to recognize the orientation and labeling of the site), the southwest corner stake of each square will be the point of reference for that square, and its *coordinates* (its identifying label) will identify that square. Thus, a square with its southwest corner stake at the datum point for the site would have the coordinates N0 W0. If the next square to be labeled for study lies from 9 meters to 12 meters north of the datum point, but has its west side along this north-south line, its coordinates would be N9 W0. (Note: These coordinates are based on the southwest corner stake's coordinates.)

If the next square to be labeled for study lies from 9 meters to 12 meters east of the north-south baseline, and has its southwest corner stake along the east-west baseline at the master datum point, its coordinates would be N0 W9. The best way to visualize this is to draw a rough diagram of a grid and label it, starting from the "southwest" or bottom-left-hand corner of your "grid." Another of the conventions that should help you keep some of this straight is to place NORTH at the top of your diagrams, grids, maps, and so forth. This helps avoid problems when others try to translate what you have written or to utilize your records in some manner.

Sometimes labels are used that do not provide this type of information. Unless there are clear and detailed explanations for where each unit is located, its size, and its orientation along some concisely measured line, these labels may be useless to other researchers. For emergency or salvage efforts, which (one hopes!) will be tied to an accurate mapping system at a later date, on occasion, letters of the alphabet may be used to designate a series of units for study—or numbers from 1 to 20, and so on. If there are five squares north-south with five additional ones adjacent to them, also running north-south and top-to-bottom, there would need to be clear explanation of how the labels ran—1–5, top to bottom, followed by 6–10 in the adjacent row—also top to bottom, or bottom to top? The same would be true for A–E, and F–J. However, these can be utilized for emergency situations, as long as they are incorporated into a more standardized mapping system. It is dangerous to assume that this incorporation will be done without loss of data or confusion of records, though. Mixing labeling systems can be problematic.

EXAMPLES OF ALTERNATIVE LABELS FOR GRIDS

North

A	F	K	P	U
B	G	L	Q	V
C	H	M	R	W
D	I	N	S	X
E	J	O	T	Y

North

A	B	C	D	E
F	G	H	I	J
K	L	M	N	O
P	Q	R	S	T
U	V	W	X	Y

North

1	2	3	4	5
6	7	8	9	10
11	12	13	14	15
16	17	18	19	20
21	22	23	24	25

FIGURE 5-2
Using a Level-All, compass, and stadia rod, students create a north-south line.

FIGURE 5-3
Three tape measures may be used to create a square.

FIGURE 5-4
Be sure to select good permanent reference points—which one is the "lone tree"?

FIGURE 5-5
Center the line level on the taut string before measuring unit depth.

FIGURE 5-6
Damage to a site from a storm may be extensive.

DIG!

Students have helped set up the grid and mark the excavation units that are to be sampled. Those surface clues have everyone excited and raring to get to work! Each student has decided where he or she wants to dig! However, a few preliminary steps remain before shovels meet dirt.

The preliminary plot map must be drawn, checked by the instructor, and placed in the record book. The surface debris must be inspected and all the artifacts—bottle caps, glass, plastic cups, and projectile points—must be gathered up and placed in an artifact bag labeled for the surface of that particular excavation unit. If the site has not been plowed or otherwise mixed extensively, each of these objects may be plotted *in situ* and labeled carefully so that each one can be mapped in the laboratory. The artifact bag, with either plotted or nonplotted materials, will be labeled with the following information on the bag. The format will be standardized for the site and is relatively standard for most archaeological projects.

Site Name

Square (Unit) Designation

Level (The first level will be "Surface")

Date

Excavators' Names/Initials

Why is it important to label in a standard manner? This procedure prevents omission of information. Also, if the label is damaged, deciphering it may be possible on the basis of what remains, if there is a predictable pattern of placement of the information. Further, long after the field work is completed, others may be using the information from the bags, and may be recording the information on computers. If consistent format is the rule, their work is facilitated. Also, if there are any questions about the materials, the date of the research, or any other factors related to the artifact bag, the date, square, level, and excavators' names may serve as clues to the location of more information in the field notebooks, the record sheets, or other documentary records of the project. Also, if the excavators are available, they may be contacted for added help.

Once the surface rubble has been inspected and the artifacts plotted, removed, and bagged, an area adjacent to the square is selected for placement of all the noncultural rubble and soils excavated from the square. This sounds simple, but several factors must be considered, such as: How close is this dumping spot to other squares that will be excavated? Is the chosen dump spot likely to be the next logical area to be excavated? Is there a prevailing wind that will blow the soil right back into the excavation if the materials are placed on that side of the excavation? How friable (loose) the rubble and soil are in the square may dictate how far from the edge of the excavation it should be deposited. No one wants to re-dig soils.

The final step before actual excavation can begin is measuring and diagramming the "floor" of the excavation site. Use of a Total Station to plot the surface contours of each excavation unit—on all four sides and across the center—would be most efficient. Why do we bother to plot this? Topography is a clue to what is buried beneath today's surface. If soils are disturbed, the direction and degree of disruption may be reflected topographically. The direction of plowing and planting may vary annually, and from one part of the field to another. Noting this may help explain decaying plant matter or other anomalies.

If the measurements are to be done manually, there is a procedure using two or three tape measures, a line level, and string. For best results, three people assist with this process. However, experienced individuals can do it with two people, or, when pressed, one person can even do it alone. At the time that the excavation units are set up, the exact elevation of the southwest corner of each square will be measured (above mean sea level). Because excavation and weather problems may modify the terrain, an arbitrary mark will be placed on the southwest corner stake of the excavation unit, at an elevation of 5/10 of a foot (6 in. or 15 cm.) above the ground surface. It is very important to be sure that the stake is stable, and that no one bumps it, decides to hammer it farther into the ground, or changes its elevation in any other manner, because it is to become the point of reference for the excavation unit.

The next step is to attach a 3-meter (more or less) string to the southwest corner stake at the mark on the stake. Attach a line level to the string and

FIGURE 5-7
At last it is time to excavate!

FIGURE 5-8
Soil differences outline plow scars and furrows—so do corn growth patterns.

center it along the string. Extend the string with its line level centered along the side of the square, with the level bubble in the center of the level. Be sure the string is taut. Measure down from the string to the surface of the excavation unit at intervals recommended by the director, and record these measurements on a diagram that is to scale for the excavation unit. As a reference point, a second tape measure may be placed along the edges of the square to indicate where each measurement is made. Repeat the procedure for all sides and across the center of the square. Although some people try to take shortcuts by listing all the locations and their measurements in columns, we have found that errors occur when the depth measurements and the horizontal locations are not recorded on the square diagram as you measure them. Measuring errors are easier to catch when they are being placed directly onto a diagram for the "floor" of the excavation.

At each stage of the procedures, the director or assistants should check to be certain that the process is proceeding accurately. Often these diagrams are initialed as they are completed. That way it is more likely that errors may be caught before the evidence needed to correct them is destroyed.

Now, finally, excavation will begin! Working from the highest corner of the excavation unit, the sod or other vegetation is removed cautiously with a sharp-edged trowel or flat shovel. The thickness of the layer removal at this stage is determined by the nature of the site itself, the density of the vegetation and its roots, and the director's insights about how much soil disturbance there may have been prior to the excavation. Skimming off and screening (sifting through 1/4-inch mesh) the surface materials will be the initial step. The first level or layer excavated often extends across high parts of the square, to create an artificially leveled, flat surface. Beginning students will measure frequently (using the same measuring technique employed to map the original surface) to check the degree of level or flatness of the excavated surface. No rocks should be gouged out; no holes should be excavated into the surface as this process occurs.

Any artifacts found will be plotted, if the soils appear to have been undisturbed previously, or bagged by level and general location, if the initial level of the excavations is deemed a disturbed one. No matter how "disturbed" the soils may be, the more accurate the locational data are, the better. For instance, noting that an artifact, or all the artifacts, appear to be within a furrow in a plowed field, and in one particular quadrant or quarter of the square under excavation, may prove to be significant later in the excavation.

Prior to the start of excavation, the director will have determined the thickness of the layers or levels to be excavated at one time. These layers or levels may be natural ones or arbitrary ones. *Natural level* refers to the different layers of soil or rock—the stratum. Since soil strata change because of the material they contain, the history of their deposition, and the location in which they are found, they tell researchers a great deal about the site. However, sometimes a stratum is very large or deep—several feet thick,

for example. Probably, its deposition took quite a long time to occur. Therefore, materials near the top, middle, or bottom (or late, middle, and early materials) of the stratum may provide significant information about the historical
development of the layer itself. Excavation of the stratum, then, should pro-
ceed in thinner slices or layers. These thinner layers within a stratum are determined by the director, on the basis of knowledge or sense of the importance
of these more subtle differences. These layers-within-layers are called *arbitrary levels*.

Whether the levels are "natural" or "arbitrary," thick or thin, the technique for their exploration and removal must be horizontal scrapes, not perpendicular gouging. Only in this way will you be able to see the changes in
soil color and actual horizontal and vertical relationships of objects found
within the stratum. There are other uses for arbitrary levels. When the nature
of soil strata is unknown, excavation may utilize arbitrary levels to determine
what the natural stratigraphy and cultural stratigraphy, if present, are.

How thick should arbitrary levels be? Depending upon the nature of the
site, excavation levels may be measured in centimeters, inches, or tenths of feet.
A common "thickness" of arbitrary levels is about 3 inches or 7.5 centimeters,
although in some cases, a larger unit is selected arbitrarily. Frequently, in sites
where the soils have been plowed, researchers still utilize a 3-inch (7.5 cm. or
0–.25 feet) arbitrary level within the plowed stratum to train students in care-
fulness and accuracy of excavation, before they reach the less disturbed subsoil levels.

Strictly horizontal levels are excavated. All depth measurements are reckoned from the square's arbitrary datum point unless the Total Station is present and can be used to record these measurements. The result, in most cases,
is that the first level in a particular excavation does not really scrape soils from
the entire square. In the areas of the square where the ground surface was
high, it has been scraped and screened; in areas where the ground surface
was lower before the excavation even began, no scraping may have occurred.

If the arbitrary first level excavated is from a high point in the square that
is as high as the arbitrary measuring point on the southwest corner of the excavation unit (based upon the surface measurements made before the excavation began), then the first level would be 0–7.5 cm. (or 0–.25 feet or 0–3
inches) below datum. By convention, this would be recorded on the artifact
bags and field notes as 0-7.5 cm. B.D. (B = below and D = Datum for the excavation unit). Thus, the level bag would say: Site Name, Square Designation,
0–7.5 cm. B.D., Date, Initials of excavators. If there are several bags of artifacts
for the level, it is wise to label this on the bag, too. Usually, "1 of 2" or "2 of
2" is the system used.

All of these bits of written information seem to include everything that
needs to be recorded, doesn't it? Well, the student field notebook needs to include even more detail. Unless everyone is using the same datum point for ab-
solutely every measurement of every location in the site, or the Total Station

FIGURE 5-9
Initial excavation may mean skimming off thin layers of topsoil with a trowel or flat shovel.

FIGURE 5-10
Features may be covered while surroundings are cleared and mapped.

is employed to measure all these measurements, it is vital to include more information in the notes. For example, which corner of the square is being used as the arbitrary datum point for the square? Sometimes, due to the topography or buried rocks or other difficulties, a different corner of the excavation unit must be used for measurement. In all cases, it is better to record the corner used, whether it is the conventional one or not. In some cases, the arbitrary point above the ground surface at the southwest corner is downslope from the surface of some portions of the unit. It is important to make that clear in the notes, and to be certain that the measurements of various portions of the excavation reflect this.

Why is all this measurement important? Meticulous care is exerted to record the depth below today's ground surface and below the site datum point, of any changes in soil color, as well as texture, rock or artifactual materials, or other features. From these data, the site can be reconstructed after it has been excavated. Relationships between soil color or textural changes may correlate with site use by humans, relationships of rocks, or artifacts. These color or textural changes may reflect camping activities, a flood episode, or dumping by glaciers. Careless record-keeping may obliterate these clues to environmental conditions, human behaviors, or relationships between these.

Once started, each arbitrary level is troweled or shoveled in the same cautious manner with all objects of "unnatural origin" left in place (*in situ*), recorded, and plotted as to horizontal and vertical location. "Unnatural origin" is an ambiguous term for something that often is just that—ambiguous. Beginning students are terrified that they will miss important objects and contexts. This concern is advantageous since it tends to make students work more slowly and carefully at this stage. Often rocks are left in place even when they may prove to be of no archaeological significance. To prevent some of the frustration and disappointment that is generated when objects or discolored soils prove to be natural occurrences with no cultural significance, several archaeological terms have been devised for these discoveries. Amongst these are "leaverite" and "nothing stone." The first refers to "leave-'er-right-where-you-found-'er" while the second is self-explanatory.

At last, the digging is happening! However, there is much more involved than merely moving soil. Soil samples are taken, in each level, for laboratory testing. Usually, these are taken with a clean trowel from the same location within the excavation unit, at the same general phase of excavation of the level each time. Partly, this is done for consistency since you want to be certain that you detect changes in the context of whatever cultural materials you find. Another reason for this is to make it a routine that will be remembered consistently. The records, and the labels on the sample containers themselves, show where, when, and by whom the samples were taken, and for what purposes.

The soil tests conducted at the laboratory include *flotation* to detect seed, bone, or shell remains; pollen analysis to detect vegetational content of the site through time; chemical analysis to detect soil acidity, phosphorus, fluorine, ammonia, and other soil ingredients, which may reflect variation in organic content; and charcoal extraction for radiocarbon dating. Often, a series of samples will be taken to fulfill these requirements, in each level. Records of these, as well as clear indications of their contexts, are vital to the research. Some of these samples require differential treatment, too. Ammonia and certain other ingredients evaporate if exposed to the air; charred organic materials are contaminated if touched or placed in containers other than uncontaminated aluminum foil, and must not be allowed to mildew. Other soil samples must be dried, somewhat, in order to prevent mold from forming. Ideally, samples are processed immediately so that some of the risks are avoided.

There is a small, conical device about 10-in. [25 cm.] long, which can be inserted into the soils to determine, at least roughly, soil acidity or alkalinity, as well as moisture content. This device may be used to check these factors each morning when the excavation begins for the day, and at the beginning of each new excavation level. Part of its usefulness is its reflection of changes in soil densities or permeability. Whenever there are anomalies in an excavation unit, it is helpful to utilize this device to see whether the visible distinctions between soils are reflected by differences in moisture and acidity.

Once these tests are completed and recorded in the field notebook, the remainder of the soil from each excavation level is removed and sifted through the screen of the mesh size deemed most appropriate to the soils of the area. All artifacts are left in place as the troweling or shoveling progresses. Many clay soils are so compact that 1/4-in. screen mesh makes the work difficult, if not impossible. On the other hand, sandy soils can be sifted with ease through 1/8-in. mesh. Sometimes soils are wet-screened through mesh of graduated sizes to make certain that beads, bits of bone, and other tiny cultural materials are not missed. This process creates many problems. Soils are washed away so they cannot be replaced in the excavation when work is completed. If soils are washed away, they are redeposited in a new location where they may be problematical, creating silt build-up in an area where it is damaging to the landscape. Also, artifacts that were missed in the troweling may be damaged or destroyed by the force of the water, and the expenditure of water may be deemed wasteful. Naturally, in very dry regions, this technique would be undesirable and probably prohibited.

The purpose of screening is to recover all the tiny fragments of cultural material that might be missed by troweling, brushing, and shoveling alone. Whatever techniques are used, screening is viewed by some as dreary, dull, and time-consuming. In some sites, however, beads, fish scales, fish bones, tiny snails, and other items can only be recovered by this process.

Invariably, the excavation process is slow, and may seem tedious, with far fewer rewards than most people expect. Of course, finding everything (*in situ*) in the excavation itself is a remarkable feat; however, since all the soils need to be screened, the screeners prefer the moments of excitement when tiny fragments of something unique appear. Some days, nothing of scientific interest appears in the excavation units or their screens. Other times, one or two squares are producing large quantities of archaeological information while the majority of excavators plod along, digging, screening, filling out endless forms, and filling sample boxes. No matter how often these excavators are reminded that non-culture-bearing areas provide information about the site size, shape, and distribution of materials and human activities of the past, these unfortunates in the "nonproductive" squares often suffer from everlowering morale and a general sense of abandonment by those focused on the productive area.. The director may tell them that the "ruby-eyed idol" (or Geronimo's Cadillac) will be unearthed the next morning, and hope that this incentive, or perhaps bribery ("We'll stop for ice cream on the way home if you finish the report sheets on time.") will carry the sufferers through these unrewarding periods of field work.

FIGURE 5-11
A buried brick walkway and scattered
"natural" rocks were excavation highlights.

FIGURE 5-12
*The soil moisture and acidity meter
is used for each level excavated.*

To make matters worse, the director often spends more time at the excavations where materials are appearing to insure the recovery of all the information that can be gleaned and less time at unproductive sites. Adding insult to injury, the "unproductives" often get the "honor" of carrying extra materials back to the van or of having to do their own work, and then having to help record some of the "glories" found by those in the other squares.

Meanwhile, the fortunate "productives" must continue with all the same procedures, recording, digging, sifting, and sampling, labeling all boxes and bags with extreme care. Tiny fragments must be packaged in such a manner as to prevent their total destruction or loss amongst larger items. Every item recovered from a level, large or small, fragile or sturdy, must be placed in a labeled container for that square and the level within it, as well as its exact location within the level, if found *in situ*, and not in the screen. There is never enough information about what is found. The motto is "more is better."

FIGURE 5-13
Soils are screened onto plastic to simplify backfilling.

Sometimes it is useful, once natural stratigraphy is evident, to shift to excavation by natural levels or strata. This is done when it is evident from earlier excavations that the cultural materials are found only in particular strata and can be differentiated clearly in that way. The approach makes it possible to clear a series of contiguous squares or blocks at the top of a particular natural stratum, and view, in the field, the "lay of the land" as it was when that stratum was exposed to the air, that is, when it represented the ground surface of that location.

That procedure worked well at the Shawnee-Minisink Site on the Delaware River in Pennsylvania, especially for the "rolling soil stratum in the Paleoindian zone" (McNett 1985, 153), where areas of more than 20 feet by 40 feet were cleared, horizontally, to expose one of the ancient occupation zones. Horizontal exposure worked well for the more recent Archaic cultural zones (Late Archaic, Early Archaic, and Early, Early Archaic), and the most recent ones just beneath the disturbed topsoil—the Woodland cultural zone at Shawnee-Minisink (McNett 1985, 6–7).

Soil sampling in natural levels may be carried out just as it was in arbitrary levels, although there may be additional samples taken where differences in the topography (high and low spots) or in color and texture suggest that the source of the soils and the manner in which they developed might be informative. R. Joseph Dent described an example of this from Shawnee-Minisink

(Dent in McNett 1985, 152–153): "The basal layers of Zone 6 mark cultural occupation of the Shawnee-Minisink site by Paleoindian populations. Silt loam soils are predominant in the zone, and it seems very likely that the basal portion of this zone is a true loess layer judging from particle percentages and distributions. Upper portions of this soil horizon contain alluvial additions that were contributed by both the Delaware River and Broadhead Creek."

At another site, the Monocacy Site (18 FR 100) in Maryland, large horizontal areas of the site were exposed, with artifacts and features *in situ*, for photographing and mapping. This work was carried out in 1967–1969; some of the more subtle clues to buried cultural horizons were not as clear in the compact clay silts of the site (Gardner and McNett 1970). However, small hearths containing soapstone-tempered pottery and charred nutshells, in one instance, and soapstone pot fragments and burned bone fragments, nearby (horizontally—no more than 15 feet away), illustrate the value of this approach to excavation. These factors made it clear that this particular habitation level showed several small cooking episodes all in close horizontal proximity. Whether they were used simultaneously or at slightly different times, is unknown.

WHAT IS A FEATURE? WHAT DO WE LEAVE IN SITU?

Any cluster of rocks that does not look "natural," any set of human-made objects, any burned soil area, any change in soil color, texture, or content, has the potential for being significant—that is, for being an *archaeological feature*. Even seemingly isolated objects may, when their surroundings are cleared through excavation, turn out to be related in some way to other adjacent objects. Again, these objects are potential ingredients of features. Special forms are set up to record different kinds of information about the clusters of materials or unnatural-seeming occurrences in the ground. Each feature of this sort will be unique and its particular characteristics will dictate what is recorded and how, and then, how it is to be excavated. Usually, a photographic record is made before, during, and after the excavation of the feature, in case certain characteristics are not noted in any other way. Often a picture or slide or segment of videotape, will reveal subtle attributes, upon close scrutiny, which may have been missed during excavation.

The little hearths and their artifactual content, at the Monocacy Site, are examples of features; a pile of animal bones or shells, exposed during excavation, are others. Ideally, all of the materials in and adjacent to the feature are left *in situ* until the entire feature-area has been exposed, cleared, and cleaned for better inspection. This provides a better understanding of what has been found and what it may tell about the people who made and used the site.

Examples of forms for recording features are in the appendix. Often the researcher adds other categories of information to the forms to fit the particular feature. Forms tend to be guidelines, not the last word in record-keeping.

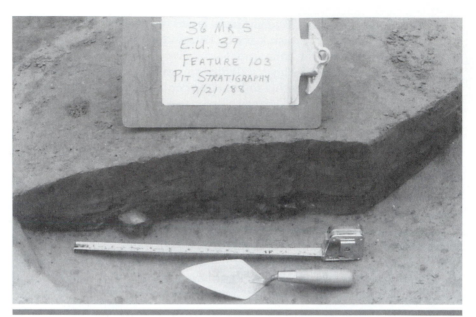

FIGURE 5-14
Varied soil patches show stages of filling when the pit was created.

HOW DO WE KNOW HOW DEEP TO DIG?

La Venta, a huge ceremonial center for the Olmec of Mesoamerica, contained buried layers of huge paving stones found 30 feet below the modern ground surface (Hester, Heizer, and Graham 1975, 132–133). Swan Point Neck, a shell field site in Maryland, where small groups of Native Americans exploited the indigenous shellfish to supplement their diet, had no artifactual materials recovered deeper than 2–3 inches below today's ground surface (McNett and McDowell 1974). The Pearson Farm and General Spaulding Pow Wow Hollow sites in Maryland and Virginia, along the Potomac River's shores, yielded all their evidence of human occupation within 1–2 feet of today's ground surface, with far more artifactual materials on today's ground surface or eroding out of the slopes (McDowell 1972). In cornfields, like the Wyns Farm Site (35 CO 30), along the Otselic River in central New York State, each year's plowing exposes artifacts that have been dislodged from their subsoil contexts. The shallowly buried pits are being truncated by modern plowing (McDowell-Loudan and Loudan 1993, 1997).

Elsewhere, all the clues to human activity may rest on the modern surface, while nearby all may be buried under tons of more recent deposition. Olduvai Gorge, Tanzania, East Africa, made famous by the late Drs. Louis

B. and Mary Leakey, has beds (strata) that are hundreds of feet thick and represent almost two million years of development—both of nonhuman primates and more recent human ancestors and their activities. The areas that have been eroded in such a way as to expose the content of these ancient strata allow researchers to find some of these remarkable buried clues to the human past. Determining how deep to dig is dependent on the rate of soil deposition in a particular place, the history of the site itself, and the types of artifactual materials that the researcher is trying to find. In some cases, excavations will go only deep enough to uncover cultural remains of one particular time period. It may be possible to recover the materials, backfill the site, and leave the earlier cultural remains that are beneath these for later research. As is the case in much research, time, money, and the interests of the researchers may be factors in the procedure that is followed.

THE BACKFILL BLUES

Once the excavations have been completed, the sites receive final scrutiny and photographing, all final soil samples are taken, and all measurements are double-checked. Ideally, this set of procedures will be gradual enough so that photographic results and all diagrams and maps have been completed, to be sure that all necessary data are in hand. Often, the time for the field season is running out and the success and completeness of records must be taken on faith.

The time has come to return all the excavated soil to the excavation. To make certain that the archaeological work will not create hazards from open holes, or poor growing conditions for future crops or gardening activities, soils should be returned to the squares in the order in which they were excavated—subsoils before topsoil. Often, to insure that future excavators will make no mistake about what was excavated previously, coke bottles or coins with the date of the year of excavation will be tossed into the bottom of the excavations. If, for some reason, backfilling is necessary but the work in those squares has not been completed, sheets of plastic or tarpaulins are placed at the base of the excavated area before the soils are shoveled on top of them to level out the land.

Almost invariably, the weather either turns unseasonably hot and humid or cold, windy, and wet when this job must be done! It requires great determination and the promise of a big "end-of-season party" to get the site backfilled completely. Other incentives may be potential course grades for the efficiency and skill with which the job is completed. A more gratifying incentive is the desire to demonstrate how well the job can be executed. Since the landowner was willing to permit excavation, it is satisfying to justify the owner's trust that the work would do little harm to the property.

When backfilling is finished, the sod may need to be replaced or seeding may be required. Often, the site soils were removed in such a way as to insure that the more fertile top soils have been kept separate for replacement in a layer over the subsoil layers, thereby insuring that vegetation will grow well. In some cases, soils and the sod have been deposited onto plastic sheeting to make sure this can occur. When excavations have taken prolonged periods, it may have been the pattern that the sod was watered and covered, so that it didn't wither and die. In cornfield excavations, if it is early in the season and excavations are completed, sometimes the corn seedlings are transplanted from new excavations to earlier ones that have been backfilled.

One certainty is that after a field crew has backfilled a site, the instructions about disposal of soils when excavating and screening suddenly make horribly good sense. The more scattered the backdirt has been allowed to get, the more difficult it is to get it all back into the holes, and the more likely it is that there will not be enough soil around to fill the excavations completely. Sometimes this makes it necessary to cart in organic debris and nearby lithic materials to line the bottoms of the excavations, so that there won't be serious depressions where excavations took place.

The writer's first field experience was in the blowing sands of Nantucket Island, Massachusetts. Backfilling consisted of dozens of backbreaking trips up and down two hills (named Mt. Everest and Mt. Kilimanjaro, on that occasion), carrying huge, smelly armloads of damp sea grass to partially fill the excavations, before sweeping in the remaining sand.

The low point of the writer's dissertation research was the purchase of thirty-three bales of straw (initially, it was to be hay, but a local farmer set the city-dwelling researcher straight about this error), to help refill the hurricane-ravaged excavations of the Fraser Site in Virginia's clay silts. Loading and unloading the straw from the poor, abused university van, and buying the straw in the first place, were most unusual experiences to be added to the credentials of a Ph.D. candidate!

In any case, the reasons for backfilling are quite logical ones. Holes in the ground tend to be unsightly and dangerous for people and other animals. One of the assurances given to those who permit archaeological research is that their land will be returned to its proper state and reseeded or sodded (if needed), if the removed sod and other vegetation have died. From another angle, erosion is an enemy to all conservation-minded people. Therefore, to prevent this problem, backfilling holes is a logical procedure.

Despite the important reasons for backfilling, it is a long and arduous task, and is not one of the favorite pastimes of the archaeological researcher or student. Therefore, when possible, backfilling is carried out in small segments. Each time a portion of an excavation is completed, it is backfilled before the next part is started. If a larger set of excavations is to be exposed simultaneously, sometimes machine-backfilling is an option. At the Shawnee-Minisink Site,

FIGURE 5-15
Backfilling after torrential rain means shoveling compact mud.

FIGURE 5-16
Two units have been backfilled and corn seedlings have been transplanted.

the threat of rain resulted in covering excavations with sheets of plastic, weighting them down with pieces of equipment, and placing all backdirt at a distance from the excavations to avoid problems of erosion. This site was machine-backfilled after excavations were completed. The shoring is evident in Figure 5-17. Even with all these precautions, erosion was a constant problem during the torrential summer rains.

FIGURE 5-17
The Shawnee-Minisink Site was covered before rainstorms. Backdirt was transported in wheelbarrows away from excavations to avoid wash-back into excavations. Machine-backfilling occurred after excavations were completed.

CHAPTER

6

THE LABORATORY

B EFORE, DURING, AND AFTER EXCAVATION, THE ARCHAEOLOGICAL LABORATORY IS a vital part of all research. Usually, to the beginner, it resembles some sort of disaster area. Once the research is under way, the clutter develops meaning and purpose.

There are some important procedures for protection of the artifacts, samples, and records, before, during, and after transport to the laboratory, however. In some archaeological projects, crew members are assigned the duty of checking in all the day's materials from field to vehicles, and then from vehicles into the laboratory. Since each crew member has worked in a specific location during the day (or several, on occasion), this person's records should indicate exactly which level bags, samples, and records have been acquired that day. These should be checked with the person handling the inventory at the vehicles, before departure to the laboratory. If there are discrepancies, this is the time to discover them and make corrections.

Everyone may be required to help transport materials from the vehicles into the laboratory, or if there are not large quantities, perhaps there will be a rotating assignment of people to help. Once in the laboratory, materials must be placed in positions that are assigned for prewashed materials. There may be a special location for soil samples, with allocations for those that must be dried, kept sealed, and so forth.

Ideally, the laboratory consists of several connecting rooms containing several sinks with heavy-duty drains, extensive storage facilities, vast refuse disposal potentials, many broad counters, tables, and chairs of appropriate height, and excellent lighting. Separate rooms should contain chemical soil-testing materials and work areas, computer equipment for cataloging and research purposes, and a telephone. Ventilation is an important consideration, too. There should be windows, exhaust fans, and first aid equipment with instructions for use. Normally, the laboratory lacks many of these characteristics. Often, it is one room that doubles as classroom and field equipment storage area for much of the year. Sometimes it is also the researcher's office and a storage location for other types of equipment.

Returning to the ideal, however, there are many additional features required for a good laboratory. It should have separate areas for "wet work," such as washing and drying artifactual materials brought in from the field, cleaning up field crew members and their tools, and, possibly, kitchen and toilet facilities. Since some types of materials, including film and certain chemicals, are best when kept refrigerated, a small refrigerator is useful.

Separate from this location, to prevent the introduction of added moisture and other impurities, there should be a relatively extensive area for cleaning and air-drying soil samples and radiocarbon samples in preparation for their subsequent submission for study by specialists. While today, most college classroom and laboratory buildings in the United States are "smoke-free zones," such things as cooking or blower exhausts must also be avoided in these rooms.

The spaces need to be large enough to permit artifactual and nonartifactual site materials from more than one site to be processed and stored at the same time, unless there are separate facilities for all the other researchers in some other location. Also, there need to be large enough sections of the facility for materials at varying stages of preparation, including those just in from the field, in-preparation scattered materials, and completed, ready-for-the-next-process stacks of objects or boxes and bags. This is true of the locations in each section of the laboratory. In large laboratory facilities, these may have permanent labels showing where each portion of the analysis is housed. More commonly, facilities will use strips of masking tape to label each area, at a specific time, indicating what is going on in that section, and at what stage.

Another essential area contains the cataloging work space, with tables, chairs, lighting, and tools for this process. Sometimes, only the artifact bags, boxes, or other containers are labeled; often, each artifact is labeled with India ink; occasionally, labels are stamped onto the objects, or stringed tags are attached to them. One system of written labels includes the following information: site code, excavation unit's coordinates, level or depth below the master datum point, or feature designation if any, date, and excavators' initials.

35 CO 30 (35 = New York State; CO = Cortland County; 30 = site #30 in the county)

N10 W20 (N10 = 10 feet north of master datum point; W20 = 20 feet west of master datum point)

1.0–1.5 feet B.D. (Level = one to one and one half feet below master datum elevation)

7/13/00 (date when artifact or level was excavated)

EM-L (initials of excavator)

Sometimes it is advantageous to add other notations to the excavation bags. After washing and sorting, for example, "W" may be placed near the bottom of the bag label; when cataloging is completed, the label may read "W/C" to indicate the stage of work completed. Other codes may be appended if they are useful and informative. If too many codes are used, the results may defeat the purpose of helping others to recognize what has or has not been completed.

FIGURE 6-1
Artifact sorting and organization patterns vary by person and materials found.

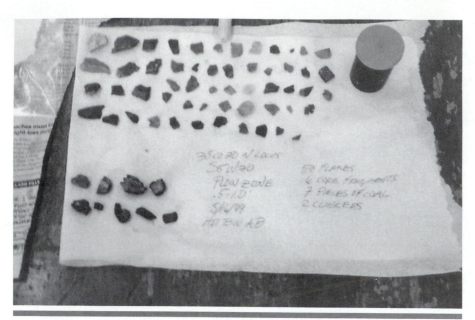

FIGURE 6-2
Here is an alternative sorting pattern for artifacts.

As in all other aspects of laboratory work, separate work stations for each stage of site material processing are needed. Usually, those who excavate particular squares or levels in them attend to the sorting of their bags, washing of the materials in them, and labeling of these materials. Other people may perform this task, though, if all the field and laboratory personnel follow the directions meticulously in labeling the artifact and sample containers with all the required information and maintain clear and accurate field and laboratory notes. If this is not the case, or even when it is, the best people to follow through on these procedures are those who have had the most experience with their own printing and their particular excavation units. In this way, they may catch and correct their own errors before these get beyond early stages of preparation for analysis.

Another isolated and specialized area needed in first-rate laboratory facilities is an area for a photographic darkroom, light tables for photographing materials, and today, equipment for digital cameras, scanners, and computer-ready equipment for processing pictures using these tools. Ideally, there will be a computer technician whose main job is to generate all these products. Here, all the film and videotapes utilized in the field and during laboratory analysis should be processed promptly and cataloged, both to give rapid feedback on the information they provide, and to warn the researchers if their equipment or film is not functioning properly. Today, video cameras, televisions, and VCR equipment for added record-keeping and viewing should be standard parts of the laboratory equipment.

Even a week's backlog in processing film and videotapes can mean disaster as far as some of the field recording is concerned. Whole sections of research may be without vital photographic records if the equipment has malfunctioned. As a case in point, in the summer of 1997, two rolls of film, placed in two different cameras, were double-exposed; believing that there was photographic backup for work done, feature excavations progressed and the chance for making a photographic record of the previous work was lost.

Elsewhere in the "ideal" laboratory, there is a storage and study area for all data sheets and mapping information in hard copy. Usually, this means a large drawing table with lights, mapping equipment, drafting tools, and storage space for maps and other papers. There should be tables and seating for personnel who are sorting and inspecting data sheets. While these facilities could be part of the computer laboratory area, neither written data sheets nor computer disks should replace one another. Not all processes work well on computers; the hard-copy backup is essential. Computers are notorious for having major failures at the most inopportune moments and data may be lost completely without this insurance. (Also, it is important that students understand what the measurements mean, so that they will recognize errors when they occur-on their own work, on the work of others, *and* in the computer-generated products!) Since all of these should be kept as dry and clean as possible, some separation of data sheets and mapping information from the washing and labeling areas is preferable.

RECORD SHEETS

Students view the data sheets and other archaeological records that are expected of them as horrifying, time-consuming, tedious, and redundant. Only later, when the search for specific information comes piecemeal from all of them, do they realize that perhaps the mass of paper work is necessary. A sample of one of the many possible sets of these data sheets is included in the appendix. It contains a level sheet, ecological data sheet, several forms for samples (soils, charcoal, and so on), feature records (not used if one does not find a feature), burial forms (not used unless burials are found), photographic record sheets, wall profile sheets (usually four per excavation unit to record the stratigraphy of each side or wall of the excavation), and floor plan diagrams (usually one of the original surface, and others for each of the stratigraphic levels excavated). In most cases, students and the site director and assistants maintain their own field notebooks that summarize everything that is going on in field and laboratory, as well as the particular highlights (or low points) of the day's work. The laboratory forms include an assortment of artifact recording sheets that contain various categories of artifacts and a number of their potential characteristics. In many cases, these forms consolidate information from the field records and add specific data learned during laboratory inspections. Sometimes, an index of codes is used to consolidate information and provide more information on forms. If it is done consistently, and if the code is available to all who may need to use the raw data, this is helpful.

THE FUNCTION OF THE RECORD SHEETS

When a site is excavated, it is destroyed—or at the very least, all the areas affected by the digging, walking, transporting of soils and equipment, and placing of equipment have been impacted by the activities. Despite excellent memories, no one remembers all the particulars of the work that has gone on in a particular excavation unit, let alone in the whole site. Often, changes in personnel during the analysis process, or even during the excavations themselves, result in a new person needing to review what has been done, how it was recorded, and what next steps were planned. Without a written record of what has already been done and what remains to be done, something may be overlooked or records may be incomplete. For example, new crew members may be asked to complete the recording of stratigraphic forms for an excavation unit. Someone may "recall" that earlier workers "finished the east and south walls, but needed to do the north and west ones." If the new workers have the data from the two finished walls, they are able to continue from these records, checking how they were done, and making certain that they are able to reconcile their measurements with those from the earlier work. Without these records, it may be necessary to redraw and re-record those walls. Worse still, if the assumption is made that the walls were drawn and recorded fully, and if the other two walls are drawn without the cross-checking, there may be missing measurements or the new data may not connect accurately with the earlier data. Frequently, once the wall profiles and photographs of the walls are done, the square is backfilled. If errors or omissions are found afterwards, it is too late!

Analysis often takes weeks, months, or even years to complete. The records become stale, memories fade, other work is injected, and field personnel scatter. Accurate and thorough records are vital for the researcher who continues the project. Years later, too, other researchers may be relying on the data provided in the records for comparative or expansion purposes. Remember, sometimes large segments of a site are left undisturbed with the hope that future research questions and future new methodology may come along for application to that site.

The Fraser Site on the Piedmont plateau of the Potomac River is an example of just this type of situation. Dr. William Harrison, an archaeologist at the American University in Washington in the mid-1960s, had excavated several test blocks at this site, in an attempt to assist avocational archaeologists who had carried out earlier testing in that vicinity. Harrison's artifact catalog, notebooks, record sheets, maps, and artifact collection data were turned over to me for inclusion with materials in my 1971–1972 excavations at the site. By 1971, many changes had occurred in the Fraser Site, and Harrison was not available to provide first-hand assistance in the field. Fortunately, Harrison kept excellent records and coded his materials in a way that made possible reconstruction of his site findings and relocation, within the Potomac River flood plain, of the areas he excavated, to a few inches! An added advantage was that I had worked with him at sites on Nantucket Island (my first archaeological field school experience).

As can be seen, all the records are vital. All the miscellaneous comments added by the excavators may turn out to be the only clue to essential features of the project that might not have been evident in the midst of the commotion of data-gathering and record-keeping during field work. Because of this, frequently, it is the student's and the researcher's field notebooks—above and beyond the forms that are supposed to contain all relevant information—that contribute something that becomes significant (and apparent) long after the field work is done.

In the laboratory, all the *wall profiles* (diagrams of the soil layers or strata including any roots, rocks, charred areas, or other anomalies that appear in the wall) may be combined in such a way as to provide a clear stratigraphic picture of the site—if they have been measured and drawn accurately in the field. All the floor diagrams (called *plan views*) of each separate cultural level may be combined to provide site-wide plot maps of the occupation or activity levels of the site. Under ideal conditions, the sheets done in the field will be so accurate that artifacts and other features that extend from one square into another will match up with one another, as drawn, forming perfect plots for the final, clean, publishable copies. Plot maps of features, ideally, should match up in the same way, so that they may be added to the site plot maps as recorded.

When these ideal conditions do not prevail, sometimes a section of the data must be excluded from the diagram. Perhaps a more thorough check of all the other data sheets and the notebooks for the units involved will clarify the situation. This extra effort could have been spent far better in actual analysis of the information collected. Meticulous and detailed work by each recorder in the first place can save loss of data, time, and patience!

Certainly, some of the data on the sheets are repetitious. However, the insurance that gaps will be filled, even when one form lacks what it should contain, is well worth the repetition. Also, sometimes during the transfer of information from one sheet to another, errors are caught! When this occurs early in the work, it may save problems later in the project.

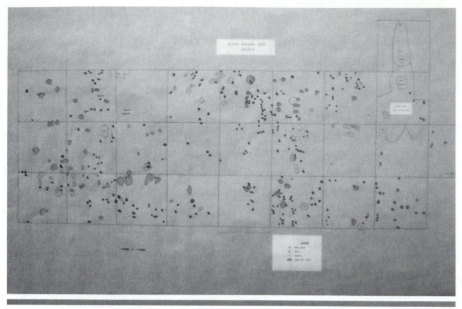

FIGURE 6-3
*The plan view shows a large set of activity areas directly beneath the
disturbed plow zone with numerous pit features, post molds, and
other indications of human behavior at the Glen Haven Site, West Virginia.*

Today, many site forms have been computerized so that all data are entered on laptop computers, in the field. However, the hard-copy backup is essential. If the computer fails, or something is omitted (or deleted in error), other sources of information are invaluable. Some of the computerized systems use codes that require skilled training; others have "user-friendly" programs that are easier to learn and to use. Unfortunately, much depends upon what is available to the particular archaeologists and their colleagues, and what is best for the type of study itself. Thus, there is variability in the manner in which records are formulated and printed. In most cases, though, the data collected and recorded are fairly similar in content.

Students use sets of flash cards to study for tests, prepare reports, and to sort during oral presentations. Some of them are coded with tabs and colored markings. This is a rudimentary, but similar system to the punch-card approach that was used in archaeology in the 1960s. Sets of cards with perforations along their top edges were punched, in a code that indicated categories of information. Then, a "needle" was used to sort those cards that contained pertinent information. The cards were more manageable than sheets of paper or notebooks full of data. This system was also in use in a number of libraries around the United States and in Canada for patron records, and in various

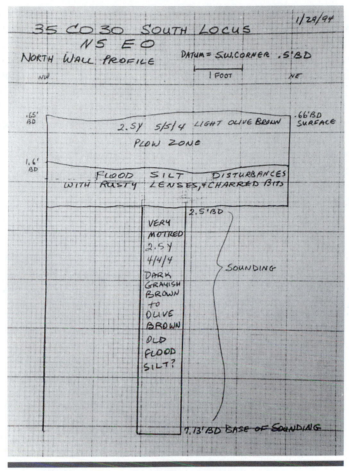

FIGURE 6-4
The wall profile shows the strata for an excavation unit.

public utilities for billing records. At that time, this approach aided in sorting out particular artifact types by their sets of attributes, and even appeared to provide slightly less bias in the selection of attributes to utilize for some kinds of analysis.

By the 1970s, though, keypunch systems had become much more sophisticated, and sets of code numbers were recorded on cards that were punched into the monster-sized computers of that time. When the system worked, and the number codes were accurate, data could be processed quickly and printed on long sheets of computer paper. The systems, Fortran IV and others, had been developed in other disciplines for a variety of purposes, and archaeologists tried to customize them to fit their needs.

It was during this period that anthropologists at many institutions, including Charles W. McNett, Jr., at the American University, were experimenting with a variety of computer programs. McNett had utilized several programs to process information from the Human Relations Area Files (HRAF) in preparing his dissertation, and was expanding his expertise into mapping and other applications to archaeology. Trial and error of this sort is essential, but extremely time-consuming and often frustrating. Also, for long periods of time, the experimentation does not appear to produce utilizable products for general usage.

However, during the excavations of the Shawnee-Minisink Site in the Delaware Water Gap, Pennsylvania (1970s), the computerized stages of data recovery and analysis produced some informative and helpful tools. McNett (1985, 23–24) summarized part of this in his credits to those with whom he conferred while setting up a system:

> The data storage and retrieval system used by the project was SELGEM, standing for "self-generating master." This program, capable of handling masses of data, had been developed by the Smithsonian Institution and was being used on other archaeological projects. Versions of the storage and retrieval routes suitable for use on The American University IBM 370-145 computer were provided by Paddy Johnson and Cynthia Irwin-Williams of Eastern New Mexico University. In addition, John Sutton of Texas Technological University provided IBM adaptations of the original Smithsonian program modules for data editing, indexing, and report writing. Reginald Creighton and Penelope Packard of the Smithsonian provided valuable technical support…. SELGEM was specifically designed to handle the large amounts of data expected to be generated by the 4 years of excavations at Shawnee Minisink. By the end of the field portion of the project, data on more than 55,000 artifacts occupied more than 325,000 card images on magnetic tape.

During the four years of the Shawnee-Minisink project, the system was modified and supplemented—with SCATERGRAM for plotting artifacts and BLOCK and CALCOMP pen plotter for line drawings (accurate to within .0025 inch [McNett 1985, 28]). Since that time, computer software companies have developed an array of programs to accomplish these goals and to make them almost foolproof (we are told). Naturally, the data typed into the computers must be accurate. The technology continues to be expensive and to require appropriate training. Another factor is that often the programs are geared to fields other than archaeology, and must be customized to fit.

With the array of computer systems and programs in use in archaeology, the student may wonder which ones he or she should become familiar with. The best approach is to see what courses are available in your local schools, especially in schools where there are anthropology programs. Then, confer with the anthropologists to see what they use, which types of consultants they use, and what basic programs they have found to be most beneficial. The Internet's numerous search engines open the door to mapping, computer illustration, and simulation programs. Often, there are special demonstration programs you can access directly and others you could order. Corel, DeLorme, Rand McNally, and other companies with mapping and other programs, provide excellent basic software to help you get started.

For explanations and some basic diagrams to help those needing to learn the mathematical parts of archaeology, I found <http://webmath.com> to be an excellent Internet site. You can also access the Web sites of many museums, colleges, and universities on the Internet, and you might like to look at the offerings of your state (or provincial) archaeological society's site, as well as those of the National Park Service, state historic preservation offices, and similar organizations. If you are interested in a particular archaeological dating method, try some of the archaeological Web sites, such as <http://www.discoveringarchaeology.com> or <http://www.archaeology.com>, and see what they have to offer. Certainly, there are more technical sources for these data, but if it is basic information you want, these would be good places to make a start.

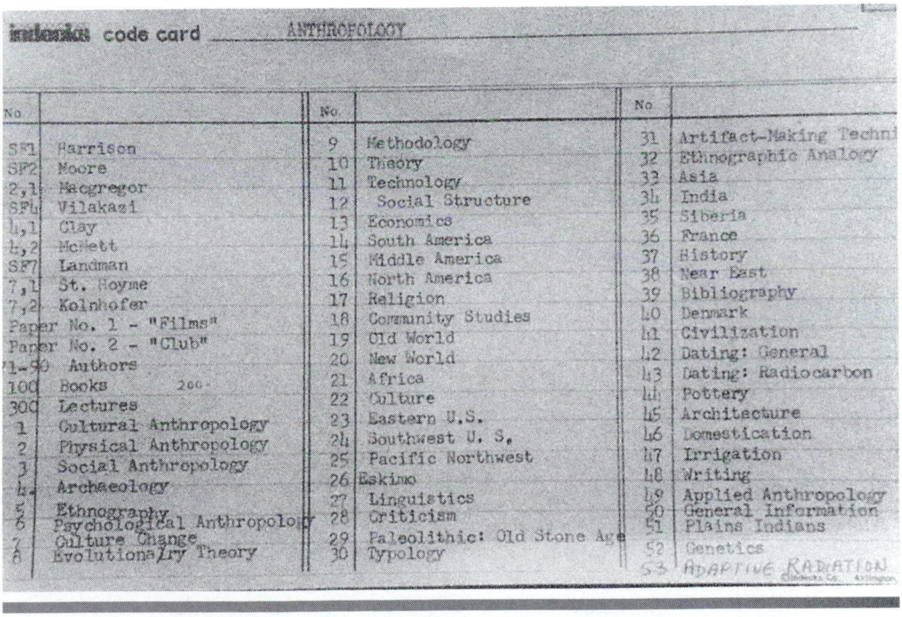

indexing code card _____ ANTHROPOLOGY

No.		No.		No	
SP1	Harrison	9	Methodology	31	Artifact-Making Techni
SP2	Moore	10	Theory	32	Ethnographic Analogy
2,1	Macgregor	11	Technology	33	Asia
SP4	Vilakazi	12	Social Structure	34	India
4,1	Clay	13	Economics	35	Siberia
4,2	McHett	14	South America	36	France
SP7	Landman	15	Middle America	37	History
7,1	St. Hoyme	16	North America	38	Near East
7,2	Kolnhofer	17	Religion	39	Bibliography
Paper No. 1 - "Films"		18	Community Studies	40	Denmark
Paper No. 2 - "Club"		19	Old World	41	Civilization
1-90	Authors	20	New World	42	Dating: General
100	Books 200	21	Africa	43	Dating: Radiocarbon
300	Lectures	22	Culture	44	Pottery
1	Cultural Anthropology	23	Eastern U.S.	45	Architecture
2	Physical Anthropology	24	Southwest U. S.	46	Domestication
3	Social Anthropology	25	Pacific Northwest	47	Irrigation
4	Archaeology	26	Eskimo	48	Writing
5	Ethnography	27	Linguistics	49	Applied Anthropology
6	Psychological Anthropology	28	Criticism	50	General Information
7	Culture Change	29	Paleolithic: Old Stone Age	51	Plains Indians
8	Evolutionary Theory	30	Typology	52	Genetics
				53	ADAPTIVE RADIATION

FIGURE 6-5
The code card shows the punch card system of cataloging data in the late 1960s.

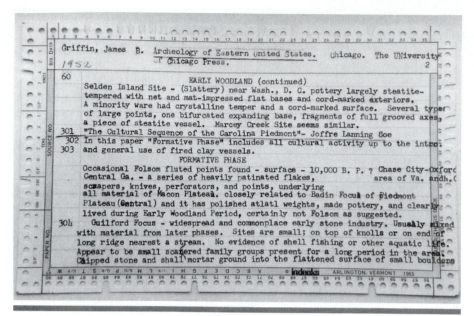

FIGURE 6-6
Here is an example of one of the punched cards using the code in Figure 6-5.

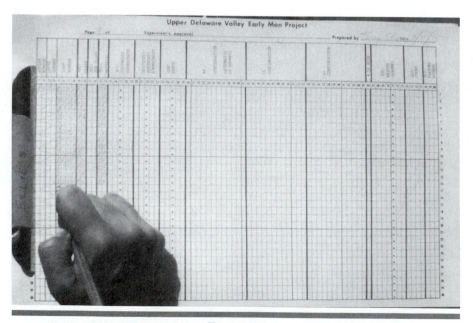

FIGURE 6-7
The data sheet was used for computerization at Shawnee-Minisink Site, Pennsylvania.

ARTIFACT BAGS AND BOXES

Over and over, accuracy and thoroughness have been emphasized as essentials in the field and the laboratory. Time and again, the researcher and students encounter errors in labeling or bags that contain artifacts or samples of some sort but have no labels at all. The horror and frustration of this cannot be underestimated. Sometimes there are distinctive objects in the artifact bags that can be traced to a particular location and particular record sheet set that might identify them. More often, they are sets of materials that might belong to any of several locations. If it is possible to retrace, with confidence, the situation that led to the error, maybe it is safe to label the wayward materials. If not, the data are lost! They become part of the "never, never land" area called *"provenience* (the exact horizontal and vertical location of an artifact, archaeological feature, or set of artifacts) unknown," virtually useless to the scientific analysis, and an embarrassment to all who were working at the site. Carelessness and poor labeling often imply that there might be even more areas of shady information. Trust and cultural significance are ethical factors of importance to reconstructing human behavior, past and present, and "maybe so" or "we believe so" have no place in the objective descriptions or data recording part of archaeological study. It is better to have excessive labeling than to have none. It is much better to pause in the midst of your work to make a label, than to continue on, placing the bag or box to one side, planning to label it later. Too many interruptions and other extenuating circumstances can make "later" never come.

FIGURE 6-8
Cover the site, pack up quickly, but label everything!

DISHPAN HANDS, EYESTRAIN, AND "WHITE-OUT" BLUES

Laboratory work may be called "unending." Often, there is little visible return for the hours of labor represented by what is done. It is essential, but due to the tediousness of some of the work, researchers sometimes feel that their student crew members are becoming careless or extremely slow. In virtually all cases, the researcher has done all the same types of work that the students are doing, and is well aware of the boredom they may be experiencing. However, the more basic sorting, washing, and cataloging that can be done immediately after each phase of the excavation—that is, in the evenings and after field work is completed for the day, or on the rainy days when field work cannot be done—the sooner everyone may begin to see what types of patterns the work is creating—or what problems or confusions or gaps are revealed by the data. Sometimes, it is not until the washing and labeling have been completed that it becomes evident that there are unique lithic materials present in one particular part of the site—in one particular cultural provenience! Elsewhere, it may be apparent, suddenly, that there are more fragments of pottery associated with wide-burned soil areas, or more definite fragments of burned shell. As excavation may be progressing at different rates in different excavation units, and as the particular excavators may not (in all cases) recognize the implications of their particular bits and pieces of evidence in the context of their isolation in digging, the laboratory opens eyes and illuminates the human behavior we all seek! Limited archaeological experience is not the only reason why cultural connections are not recognized immediately. Sometimes everyone is startled to see particular sorted piles of debitage, or pottery sherds, or bits of metal and glass, or even projectile points and other stone tools, that were encountered, plotted, mapped, and photographed in the field, only to show much more about their relationships to one another as they lie drying on the tables in the laboratory, in proximity to one another. This is when many discover archaeology for the first time. Suddenly, the purposes and relationships of objects, geography, geology, and history may make sense at last!

After the first anticipation and the first encounters with the "goodies" from the field wear off, the cleaning and sorting process may become monotonous. Since this may lead to inattention to important detail, a variety of tasks may be scheduled so that jobs are rotated among the crew. While this may seem like a wise idea, sometimes it requires increased vigilance to make certain that procedures carried out by one person are consistent with those of the others. Something as simple as the placement of labels for objects being washed, dried, or sorted may turn out to be ambiguous to the next worker. Although each level bag has its contents washed separately from all other materials, errors may occur, if the artifactual materials are scant and several bags are washed and placed for drying in too close proximity to one another. Alternatively, if there are large quantities of artifactual materials, too many artifacts may be crammed into the spaces. There may be other types of losses of information—or even materials—as well.

FIGURE 6-9
Careful separation and labeling of artifacts during cleaning is essential.

Washing artifacts may sound straightforward. However, special attention should be devoted to cleaning each object without changing the characteristics of the artifact! Pottery, scrubbed too hard, may gain markings that come from a scrub brush or a fingernail used to remove dirt from a crack, or it may lose its decoration, color, or significant wear markings. Clues about what was stored in a vessel or cooked in it, may be lost through careless scrubbing for the sake of scrubbing!

Today, it is common for artifacts from undisturbed contexts like features to be removed from the feature with plastic or latex gloves, and bagged separately for analysis of any trace chemicals or oils that may hint at how they were used and for what purposes. If this is not done, the artifact may be washed carefully, again, avoiding any scratching or altering of its surfaces, and air-dried for analysis. Determination of the degree of previous contamination must be evaluated in the field before excavators handle the objects. It would be too late to do this after materials have reached the lab, in most cases.

As noted previously, some laboratories have screened drying racks that may be stacked or shelved in some way during drying. However, if the materials are stacked, the top shelves should be loaded first since the lower levels receive all the drips from the upper ones, making drying a slow process. An essential reminder is that the level bag, with all the information recorded on it, must be kept with the drying, unmarked artifacts. Bags must not get wet or they may blur, or if they are to be used for storage later, they may mildew in storage. Even momentary carelessness can confuse the artifacts and their appropriately labeled bags. Under no circumstances should you assume you will remember what bag goes with which drying rack material!

The labeling of artifacts is another painstaking process. All artifacts must be sorted by size so that objects too small or fragile for labeling are placed in containers labeled with all the provenience information. The larger objects are labeled with all the information, using pen and India ink, covered with a layer of colorless butyrate dope (a colorless shellac-like material that will prevent the label from fading or chipping off of the artifact). If the artifact is a color on which the black ink will not take or will not show, a layer of white dope is applied first, allowed to dry, and then, the artifact is labeled, allowed to dry, then covered with the colorless dope. Any materials that have proven to be of no cultural significance now that they have been washed and inspected are discarded before labeling, in most instances. As can be seen, this is time-consuming. The dope refuses to dry, the ink smears, heads ache, and eyes burn. Needless to say, good ventilation of the room where cataloging occurs is essential.

In some laboratories, and with some types of artifacts, a permanent-ink stamping device with consecutive numbers may be utilized to catalog each artifact. While this may be useful and less time-consuming than the previous system, many artifacts are too small or too fragile to mark in this manner. Further, these devices tend to have sets of numbers on them, and would not include other types of information, such as site designation, excavation unit, level, or feature number. For the most part, this type of labeling system is limited to designation of a set of surface materials for which there is little or no provenience. Only the catalog for the site itself would include details corresponding with the numbered object.

There is an advantage to the more elaborate system of artifact labeling. In the event that objects become separated from their level bags, or from their site, for that matter, the sets of codes for site, excavation unit, depth or feature, and so forth, should aid in the return of the object to its rightful context. Another advantage is that when you want to compare and contrast the objects by laying them out for closer scrutiny, the labels ought to make this a procedure that will not create any confusion about their origins and their exact geographic relationships in the site.

Other important factors in this procedure include being certain not to cover areas on the artifact that may be important for microscopic analysis. Also, objects that may receive chemical analysis will not be labeled in this manner, in most cases. Flake or edge scars on lithics, pottery designs and markings of wear, and the fracture-planes of pot sherds are examples of areas to be avoided during labeling. Also, the labels must be legible and should be as small as possible so that when the objects are photographed, more than the label shows!

Another obvious, but sometimes overlooked, point concerns drying the artifacts. Before labeling, thorough drying of the artifacts is vital to prevent labels from peeling or smearing or sticking together in the storage container. Finished materials, those washed and labeled, are stored on shelves or tables, preferably by site, excavation unit, and provenience, for ready analysis. Frequently, since all of these steps in the laboratory processes take time, there will be codes added to the containers as each step in the analysis has been completed. Since the final step in these basic preparations for the "real, significant analysis" is to have all these basic parts completed, the containers may have the following codes on them: W = washed; C = cataloged, labeled, and recorded on record sheets; W/C = weighed/counted (for certain materials like fire-altered rock); and, OK = final check by the director.

STORAGE AND DISCARD

At various stages along the way, from excavation through analysis, some of the materials recovered from the site may be discarded. Especially in the initial days of field work, beginning students, and sometimes more experienced participants, may collect objects, generally lithic materials, that look peculiar and might reveal some previous human usage. Once they are in the laboratory, washed, and given closer scrutiny, their true nature—as "leaverights"—becomes clear. These materials must be disposed of in some way. Sometimes they can be returned to the backdirt piles beside the excavations. Other times, it is easier to dispose of them at the laboratory itself. In some cases, there is no problem with this debris. It can be tossed outside to join gravel in an adjacent parking lot. Other times, there must be special arrangements made for disposal. As a case in point, the refuse from one set of sites on the Potomac River is distributed in the basement window wells of one of the American University buildings for added drainage. Other materials became part of rock gardens and fill at the edge of University property. This only transpired after janitorial staff discovered that waste-basket-loads of gravel, dumped by them into garbage-crushing machines, damaged the machinery. This unhappy result caused anger and tension between the Department of Anthropology and the maintenance personnel. This could sound amusing if it were not destructive and an ongoing problem of archaeological laboratory analysis in most settings. No matter how or where refuse is discarded, be sure site notes and artifact inventory sheets mention things that were recorded and then discarded!

When washing artifacts, an amazing amount of mud comes off, becoming suspended in the water, and then settling to the bottom of cleaning containers. If the cleaning container is a sink or a bucket dumped into the sink, the drains will clog. If there are heavy-duty drains, there may be no major difficulties (or so I have been told). However, in most cases, after the first flooded laboratory or blocked drain, it becomes evident that heavy sludge will not go down the drain properly. What do you do with it? Sometimes, preliminary washing of artifacts can occur using buckets and water from a river or stream at the site. If the water flow is strong enough, there may be no major silt build-up problems. Otherwise, if the washing must be done in the laboratory, some procedure must be dreamed up to dispose of the silt. If there is not too much, sometimes the mud can be poured in campus or laboratory flower beds, or in the gravel driveways. Sometimes, there are outdoor heavy-duty drains that can be used. This may be another tactical and seemingly nonarchaeological problem relating to laboratory work that needs to be worked out in advance, however.

SAMPLE-DRYING AND PREPARATION FOR TESTING

All the soil, charcoal, seed, and other types of samples must be dried to prevent mildew or decay of their containers and the materials themselves. This requires several days, or even weeks, of open containers and some assurance that no contaminants will permeate or drop into them. It is preferable, despite the assurance from some radiocarbon-testing laboratories to the contrary, that cigarette, cigar, pipe, and wood smoke and ash be kept out of the area. Probably, from time to time during drying, the samples will require shaking in a manner that will shift moist materials into a position where the air can get at them.

As usual, there are exceptions to this. Samples taken for testing the presence and absence of appreciable amounts of ammonia and phosphates that might indicate human excrement (feces) or other human-related materials, should be kept sealed and should be tested immediately after removal from the site, according to Dr. James Swinehart, Professor of Chemistry at SUNY Cortland. These materials will evaporate from a sample that has been exposed to the air. Therefore, it is vital to determine in advance of any planned testing just what it is that particular laboratories and researchers require for successful testing of materials.

Charcoal samples, in some cases, can be prepared for shipping to the testing laboratory by washing in tap water or distilled water (opinions vary by laboratory), making sure that the container and drying area are free of all other soils or contaminants (including soaps). These samples are kept with their labels while they dry. Then, the resultant sample will be weighed, then packaged carefully with label, weight, context of the sample, date processed, name of processor, and any other information the particular laboratory requires.

The cost of sample testing for radiocarbon dating is about $200 per sample, and a sample must weigh at least one ounce. Extreme caution must be exerted to prevent contamination or loss of the samples or data about their context. Despite all this care, some samples of charcoal turn out to be impossible to date accurately. It is essential to submit several samples, preferably from different *loci* (places) in the same site, different cultural or stratigraphic levels, with the same cultural associations of artifacts and features, for independent testing. If possible, and if it is deemed essential, samples may be sent to two different laboratories for independent testing and cross-checking. Then, if the resulting dates are consistent with one another, there is a higher degree of reliability of the date.

Normally, the various soil samples of other types are dried, then sent with accompanying information to the prearranged soil testing laboratories for analysis. Often, these laboratories prefer to have the samples sent to them more or less "as is" for their studies. It is important to confer with the analysts in advance when possible, to determine which tests are most informative for archaeological purposes, what these entail, and how much each of the tests will cost. Sadly, the cost factor may be a top consideration for the types and numbers of tests that will be run. If this is the case, learning what the laboratory personnel recommend for storage of other samples for potential testing at a later date is useful.

Between 1920 and 1940, William A. Ritchie, a New York State archaeologist whose work has been invaluable for all Northeast United States archaeological study, excavated numerous sites, and saved an assortment of materials that many others of his time would have discarded. As a result of this, when radiocarbon dating was invented, samples from sites Ritchie had excavated were tested, yielding dates that have been correlated with many others throughout the region. His care and forethought underline the importance of saving samples of materials for future reference. One hopes that such seemingly unimportant samples include materials that may prove informative some day.

THE FIELD NOTEBOOK AND SAMPLE RECORD SHEETS

The following (on pages 108–109) is a fictional example of the information that should be found in each student's field notebook. There will be variation in format and content for particular days, but basically, the types of information shown in the example are important. Earlier discussion of notes referred to some of these factors. Standardized layout will enable others who need to use the data in the notebook to locate it easily. Definitely, pages should be numbered, at the top (left or right), so that later notes can refer back to earlier materials by page. The notes are on the left (lined) page, with excavation diagram on the right (graph paper) page.

(1)   **35 C0 30 (or laboratory)**   **6/28/97**

Met at van at 8 A.M., sunshine, 70 degrees F., no one late or absent. Departed at 8:05, after extra level bags and a bucket were collected from the lab. We saw 3 deer on Route 41, just before the turnoff to Route 23. Road construction caused a 5-minute wait while one-way traffic from the east headed toward Cortland.

Reached site at 8:50 A.M.; it's my turn to carry the heavy green bag of supplies.... No change in excavations, although raccoon, deer, and bird tracks in and around the excavations showed their curiosity about what we were doing, and maybe indicated that they drank from the dew on top of the plastic sheets covering the excavations—it's been pretty dry for the past two weeks.

Crew: I'm working with _____, in Square N105 E 5; _____ and _____ are in N100E20, and _____ and _____ are in N100 E 30. After distributing equipment and placing all general supplies in the staging area, we removed plastic, and rescued two wee frogs from our square. After arranging the screen, moving some of the backdirt farther away from the edge of the excavation, and labeling the artifact bag for today's starting level, we took moisture and soil PH readings, cleaned off the PH meter, and passed it to the others. Our readings didn't vary from those taken yesterday. We hope that means we are accurate, the meter is working, and that there will be significant changes as we excavate in deeper levels or elsewhere in the site— maybe it would be significant?

Instructions: Excavate N105 E5 with trowel, keeping all artifactual materials *in situ*, and screening all soils through our 1/4-inch mesh screen. Our starting level for today is 1.5–1.75 feet B.D. (Our square datum is the southeast corner because a deer stepped on the southwest corner, dislodging the stake and crumbling the wall.) Since we began this level yesterday, taking a soil sample, we won't take one before we begin today. If we are lucky, we may finish this level before lunch, and manage to start 1.75–2.0 feet B.D. It is below 1.75 feet B.D. that we think there may be much clearer evidence of the burned fire pit found adjacent to this excavation unit in N 105 E0.

Noon: LUNCH! We didn't manage to finish 1.5–1.75 feet B.D., but we did find and plot *in situ* three chert (light gray) retouch flakes and four unmodified (we think) river cobbles, each one more than 4 inches in diameter. Since there were similar cobbles associated with Feature 1 (see notes page ___, and feature report sheet) in N 105 E0, we are psyched!

Two visitors appeared at the site at noon, so the director had to delay her lunch to give them a tour and explain what we are doing and why it's significant. They were unimpressed by our flakes and cobbles even when we explained what we thought they meant. Since these visitors are known to be collectors of surface artifacts from sites, we hope this will discourage them from picking up materials from the surface here. They did show us materials they have collected here in the past—How do you look at, note, and record the information without seeming to be enthusiastic about people who are doing uncontrolled surface collection? The director gave the "usual" pep talk about the value of controlled study of sites, but had to avoid direct criticism since the result of it often is site vandalism and resentment. We got the "public education lecture" and were urged to share it with others, later in the afternoon (as usual!). It's frustrating to see pot-hunter collections, and know that some dig in sites to increase their yield, often recording when, but not where, they dug! Hmm!

After lunch, the sky clouded up—thunder—we're out of here. The site had to be closed, equipment loaded quickly, and we returned to the lab.

2:00 P.M.—Laboratory—everything had to be carted into the lab from the van. Unfortunately, with all the mud we tracked in and the wetness of all the artifact bags, it was disorganized and some crew were annoyed with the "sloppies" on the crew. There was an unlabeled bag of soil in the bottom of an artifact bucket—no one wanted to claim it, and it appeared to have been in the bucket for a couple of days. Time was lost while everyone checked their notes and their own excavation materials for the past three days, to try to figure out where the sample belonged.

4:00 P.M. To change the atmosphere and set the stage for tomorrow's work, "The Great Fearless Leader" showed slides, just back, from last week's work. At least these demonstrated that we are improving in our excavation techniques. We even laughed at ourselves a bit. The group mood was a bit better—especially when the sun came out!

—really didn't feel we learned much that was new today, except that we are all edgy and that "outsiders" are even harder to convince of the meaning of archaeology than we students are.

Tomorrow, we are supposed to finish up the 1/75-2.0' B.D. level—with strict instructions to FIND THAT IMPORTANT FEATURE WITH THE DIAGNOSTICS IN IT!

Note: Don't forget a pencil with a point and a new pack of Kleenex for tomorrow!

ANALYSIS AT LAST!

ANALYSIS, FOLLOWED BY SUMMARY AND CONCLUSIONS, ARE THE CLOSING PARTS of a research project. Some refer to this as the answer to the question "What does it all mean?" Often, this part of research appears to outsiders as the easiest part. However, to the researchers themselves, it looms as a formidable task! The time has come for all the parts—all the kinds of data gathered, all the questions that have been asked, all the fragments, ideas, puzzles, successes, and failures—to be placed into some sort of meaningful order. In any research project, one starts with a question or hypothesis to test. This is the day of reckoning—has the question been answered? Was the hypothesis supported? Were the procedures and data-gathering adequate to the task?

All the excavation, mapping, washing, sorting, labeling, and general organization of materials is finished. It is time to group what has been found into the sets of categories that will illustrate how and why the research has been a success. There should be patterns. Are these patterns relevant and appropriate to what you seek?

What types of data, and how many of them, have been collected? Is everything made of one raw material or several? What varieties of shapes and sizes are represented? What *volumes* (how many specimens of each) are in the inventory? Would it be more meaningful to weigh some of these materials instead of counting them? Many different kinds of forms have been filled out; all artifacts have been counted—perhaps they have been counted in diverse ways—by material, size, color, shape. Categories for excavation units and levels within them have been separated. The information about materials that have been weighed, counted, and singled out as something of special importance have been sorted; notations have been made (from time to time, as they occurred to the researchers) as aids to understanding what the categories might imply. Do these incidental thoughts have relevance to the total picture?

Perusal of some of the forms used and notes in field notebooks reveals questions the researcher asks of all the data. The artifact inventory sheet, for example, lists six fairly specific categories plus a miscellaneous column for things that do not fit elsewhere. These categories are most relevant for New World archaeology, especially archaeology relating to the pre-European-contact artifacts. Elsewhere, and for other time periods (European colonial periods, for example), the nature of the artifacts might dictate different labels. The feature and burial report sheets, coupled with the maps, artifact inventory sheets, and all the other records of these particular places and occurrences, indicate what sorts of data are to be correlated in these cases. Quantities in numbers, weights, and percentages of things, materials, and debris may prove to be extremely significant. These must be recorded if this has not been done during the cataloging process. Often at this stage, researchers will discover obvious omissions in what has been recorded—or inconsistencies in the recording process. While this may not occur quite as frequently in cases where computer-generated forms serve as a reminder of what needs to be included, and may even prompt the researcher to add certain data, human error may creep in despite this reminder.

A major focus of attention, as is evident from this list, is detail. An important feature of the detail is determination of interrelationships among the details. Callahan (1974) and Gross (1974) have demonstrated that there can be vital lessons in technology learned from close attention to details of lithic debitage (waste flakes and shattered fragments). When a stone tool-maker is manufacturing something, there will be a set of tools for making tools, a "mental template" (Deetz 1967) of what the finished product will look like, and a set of phases through which the object will pass before the product is completed. Gross succeeded in plotting the distributions of lithic debitage for the various stages of the activity at the Thunderbird Ranch Site in Virginia (see the National Park Service publication of *Common Ground*, spring/summer 2000, for illustrations of the site and artifact plotting). Further, Gross demonstrated the most likely shifts in body position of the manufacturer as these stages proceeded, correlating them with the patterns of distribution of these lithic fragments at the site. Here, due to his familiarity with the activities and careful attention to detail, the human activity of stone toolmaking could be reconstructed in far greater detail than is common in analysis of lithic materials. The more frequent approach has been to plot the distributions of such materials and merely indicate the "beginning, intermediate, and finishing areas" of such materials. Wheat (1967) has demonstrated similar detail and human choice in the killing, preferential butchering, and eating of bison. His detailed plotting of wind direction, site topography, and bone and artifact distribution has caused the hunting knowledge of his archaeologically known group to become far more clearly understood—and perhaps, more respected—than had been the case previously.

Analysis is far more complicated than this description. To reach the interpretations and inferences cited here, one must examine every item recovered as an independent as well as a dependent or interdependent part of the whole picture of human activity. Words and diagrams must be employed to provide a clear, concise description of what has been found. Caution must be exerted to use words and diagrams that will be meaningful to the reader as well as the analyst. One is not merely reporting; one is attempting to produce as complete a picture of the excavated (and destroyed) site and its inhabitants as possible, and to follow through with interpretive statements that will make the past human population of the site contribute to our knowledge of their time and behavior. Ideally, we want the site to "come alive." However, it is dangerous to be too romantic or dramatic about this because the imagination may be vivid in ways that are misleading.

The type of detail alluded to here can be seen in the analysis of chipping waste or lithic debitage. Many articles and books demonstrate some of the procedures followed to generate this material. Wilmsen (1968; 1973; 1974), Bordaz (1968), Bordes (1968), Callahan (1974, and others), Crabtree (1972), and many others have worked for years to perfect their techniques, insights, and utilization of these to understand the archaeological evidence through their experimentation. Their efforts have produced a vast inventory of valuable information for the lithic analyst. One strikes a stone with stone, bone, antler, or wood; the first stone fractures in a distinctive way, reflecting what type of stone it is, how, and at what angle it was struck, and by what tool it was struck. Repetition of this process, with variations, will produce somewhat predictable *fracture patterns* (breaks) and identifiable fragments of flaked or shattered lithic refuse. If a pointed tool (bone, wood, metal) is pressed against a thin, tapered, stone surface, with the right pressure and angle of force, equally recognizable fragments, or "pressure flakes" will be removed from the thin surface, creating a serrated or irregular, sharp edge.

Thus, the lithic analyst looks at all the lithic material from a specific stratum in a site, separates it into particular kinds of stone, kinds of flakes, tools, cores, shattered bits, and so forth, counting each of these categories. Then the analyst tries to determine who was doing what, where, why, and how. Of course, the exact locations of every one of these artifacts must have been plotted and must be kept in mind as these sorting processes take place. The analyst cannot question the toolmaker, nor can the processes be observed to see whether the particular mannerisms or techniques inferred are "true." The researcher must look at the refuse found, where it was found, and try to make best guesses about the toolmaker's procedures.

In an area of the Potomac River Piedmont plateau, an interesting but elusive pattern of stone toolmaking began to emerge from an approximately two-mile segment of the shoreline. Represented by four or five sites, I believe the artifacts represent the Archaic period of cultural development (stone projectile points, flake scrapers, bifacially flaked knives, and the absence of any pottery or hints of domesticated plants are hallmarks of this period in the Middle Atlantic seaboard states of the United States). A distinctive type of fine-grained tan quartzite had been utilized to produce what appeared to be carefully percussion-flaked and pressure-retouched blades. Elsewhere along the Potomac, in Archaic sites, somewhat similar blades were found, but they were made of flinty rhyolite (McDowell 1972). It was this writer's belief that these sites might represent a set of interrelated activity areas utilized by particular groups for their varied subsistence activities. The four or five sites with the distinctive quartzite blade-like tools reflected different types of human activities—hunting and nut-gathering, flood plain camping and fishing, and collecting of wild plants within a very limited area—and reflected activities of one family unit with specific sets of tools in their tool kit. Due to the nature of the quartzite used, wear marks are not defined clearly on the blades, nor can their specific functions be determined with reliability from their contexts. They would be useful for cutting with some sawing action because of the fine-grained but granular texture of the stone, but more evidence of use is needed.

What seems to be significant here is that a particular lithic material, of the range available in the region, had been selected for use in the manufacture of these blades. Their manufacture seemed to reflect remarkable attention by the craftsperson to the details of the craft and precision in its execution, despite the gritty, unpredictable nature of quartzite as a flaking material.

Similar tools of rhyolite show this type of precision, but the lithic material is far more conducive to success than is quartzite. Elsewhere up and down the Potomac River, where this and other qualities of quartzite and quartz are used for tool manufacture, far less precision in the manufacture of tools and blade-like objects has been noted. The writer's impression is that one toolmaker might be responsible for the particular set of blades from these seemingly related sites and that this type of clue, as well as others of technological nature, should provide an important direction of research for future archaeologists. Also, since 1972, major strides have been made in the study of lithics and the possible chemical or organic residues that might be on the surfaces of tools. Although the ones studied along the Potomac in the early 1970s may have been scrubbed, rubbed, and touched with bare hands too often for these tests to be possible, perhaps similar discoveries in other areas will shed light through this type of analysis.

A list of some basic attributes or traits for study of lithic artifacts might include identification of lithic material, artifact length, width, thickness, general shape, edge angles, wear-marking evidence, if any, details of flake scars on the object, grinding, polishing, whether it is broken or whole, any staining or other types of characteristics, and of course, its location and context. These, and any other kinds of information, including nearest source of the raw material, percentage of this type of material as opposed to other lithic materials at the site, and so on would be part of the analysis. Microscopic analysis to detect minute details could be significant. Many of these types of studies might begin in the field with photographs of the object *in situ*, and its removal with sterile gloves to a sterile container for laboratory analysis by specialists in search of possible clues to plant or animal tissue on the object. If the artifacts have been contaminated by hands or other means, this should be recorded; a determination of the degree of damage done might be gained from the chemical analyst.

Intensive studies of ceramics, bone, and all other materials from the site would occur in like manner. The specialists' reports on soils, radiocarbon dating, residues from pits, and so on will be added to all the other data to help interpret the organic content of areas of the site. This may reflect various types of human or other animal wastes, in some cases, as well as the age of the cultural behaviors and human events represented at the site.

Ideally, it may become evident that particular individuals were using specific types of objects. Traditionally, assumptions have been made about cooking, cleaning, and child-rearing activities as women's work, and hunting, toolmaking, heavy construction, and major ritual activities as men's work. This may be valid in some instances, but, possibly, more subtle indicators of gender relationships might be teased from the data with careful scrutiny and some cautious ethnographic analogy. Perhaps those who worked with particular herbs, wove baskets, and carried out much of the curing activity could be documented as the same group members who were engaged in child care, cooking, and cleaning activities within particular localities within the site. An absence of weaponry or toolmaking equipment and debris from this locality might suggest that the males and females had sex-related work areas.

Correlation of all this information into a coherent picture of the site and its people is the next step. All the descriptions and evidence will be presented. Similarities and differences between these data and those elsewhere will be discussed for comparison and contrast and the implications of these.

Finally, a general interpretation of the meanings of all the descriptive data will be compiled, consolidating all that is known into a coherent picture of the cultural patterns reflected by the site. Questions that have been answered by the research, as well as those left unanswered by the study, are noted, and a final summary of the site's contributions to the understanding of human behavior is given.

All of these data will become the content of a site report of the particular research project. These reports are vital portions of the information bank for a particular area and for particular research emphases for others elsewhere. Often, they are useful for totally different areas of the world as helpful research designs and for comparative and contrastive data.

CHAPTER

8

ARCHAEOLOGY TODAY: THE BIG PICTURE

THE BEGINNING OF THE TWENTY-FIRST CENTURY SEEMS TO MARK A TIME OF REVISING and rethinking many things, including archaeology. While much previously gained information and many aspects of traditional methods and theories continue as underpinnings of the study of human beings, there is concern that we not stagnate or refuse to consider alternative viewpoints and methodologies, including those of diverse ethnic groups. While this is not a rejection of previous efforts in archaeology, it is a time for selection, modification, redefinition, and development of a new composite of segments from earlier efforts in and peripheral to archaeology.

Reviewing some of the earlier efforts and strategies in the field of anthropological archaeology, we are impressed by the systematic manner in which Thomas Jefferson, as early as 1784, excavated an Indian mound. He wrote copious notes on the sequence of strata and the location of the mound, including details of its natural and cultural setting. It was he who recognized that Native Americans, not some group of outsiders from Egypt or the Middle East, had created these remarkable structures. (Jefferson 1801 in Wheeler 1954, 58). Others who have provided some of the underpinnings of our work are the stratigraphers and naturalists of the 1800s who demonstrated independently that what Jefferson said about stratigraphic sequences was correct. Many antiquarians, collectors of art objects and suppliers of museums' displays, provided materials that led to our kinds of archaeological research. Unfortunately, the objects they provided were taken out of context, but the catalogs and laboratory analyses devised for the study of these objects have proven to be useful for some aspects of theory formation and discussion. Certainly, some of the ideas and theoretical formulations were misguided and incorrect (Eliot Grafton Smith's incredible theory of the diffusion of major features from Egyptian "civilization" to the Malay Peninsula, Mexico, and elsewhere, and the endless inventories of individual features that were traced without any direct evidence—geographically, temporally, or socioculturally, for example (Hoebel 1966, 518; Fagan 1999, 16). Extreme applications of certain ideas, such as unilinear (one line, with an inevitable sequence of cultural developments from stage to stage) evolution and diffusion (like Eliot Grafton Smith's) do not destroy the utility of these concepts for archaeology and its parent discipline, anthropology. Rather, they serve as reminders that continuous rethinking and revision are essential in any field of study, as new information and new insights appear. Augustus Lane Fox Pitt-Rivers, a British general, made "evolutionary" sequences of guns and other weaponry, from simple to complex, from old to young, in the late 1800s. As another hobby, he directed and recorded extensive archaeological excavations in which all artifactual materials were mapped three-dimensionally, in an effort to gather data, trace structures and settlement patterns, and devise artifact "evolutionary" typologies (Wheeler 1954, 13, 18, 25; Fagan 1997, 26–27). Heinrich Schliemann, an amateur reader of the classics (in the 1860s and 1870s), despite horrific field techniques, even compared with certain other contemporary excavators, contributed to our knowledge. He utilized ethnohistoric and mythological data—written records including *The Iliad*—to determine the probable location of Troy, and to attempt to excavate it (Hole and Heizer 1973, 53–54; Fagan 1999, 10–11). His methods reflect what we continue to value—the application of scientific method—in that Schliemann utilized a problem-oriented approach to his data!

Other important additions include W. W. Taylor (1948), who drew attention to the flowering of many new approaches to the study of archaeology, and recommended the full exploitation of these and more in what he called a "conjunctive approach" to the study of the human past. Joseph Caldwell (1958) utilized Taylor's holistic approach to formulate a model for subsistence patterns and their development through time within a geographic-cultural area. Willey and Phillips (1958) formulated gross stages that offer a framework for the entire prehistory of the New World. Building on these are a series of settlement pattern–procurement pattern studies and cries for more in both the Old and New World. Patty Jo Watson, Lewis Binford, Sally Binford, Richard MacNeish, Kent Flannery, Bruce Trigger, Fred Plog, Stuart Struever, Robert Braidwood (to some extent), Margaret Weide, and William Longacre, are representative of these types of approaches. In all of these cases, there is an increased use of a multitude of specialists from other disciplines, and the application of new techniques. Technological developments, using an array of computer-related offerings, digital cameras, scanners, camcorders, and specialized films, have transformed archaeological research in other ways. A. C. Spaulding, Edwin Wilmsen, C. W. McNett, Jr., Dean Snow, and J. W. Michels are examples of researchers who have experimented with these types of equipment. In particular, Spaulding and Wilmsen used computer programs for quantifying a number of artifactual types; McNett applied computer approaches to the Human Relations Area Files (HRAF) for correlating cultural traits around the world as well as for recording and manipulating archaeological data from the Shawnee-Minisink site. Snow and Michels have applied plotters and graphing programs to population data for early Iroquoian sites. Many of their approaches are statistically and demographically oriented. David Clarke (1968 *Analytical Archaeology*) represents British and American scholars who have developed systems analysis in archaeological contexts. Studying archaeological sites as sets of economic, social, and ritual functional units that are part of a system is his perspective.

An endless list of names and specialized efforts could be added here, but the following individuals represent them. Graham Clark is well known for presenting overviews of Old World cultural sequences and technological and subsistence explanations of these, Stuart Piggott worked along similar synthesizing lines, and Vere Gordon Childe is best known for his ecologically based evolutionary stages of cultural (especially technological) development from earliest human activities to the "industrial revolution." Childe envisioned changes in human behavior as dependent upon the degree of energy under human control. When animals were domesticated and farming began, archaeological sites reflected major changes in location, size, and content. It was his belief that location had much influence over what people did and how much success they had economically. Methodologically, Sir Mortimer Wheeler, another British archaeologist, spelled out the techniques and purposes of archaeology; the late Louis B. and Mary Leakey, as well as their son, Richard Leakey and his wife, Meave Leakey, have searched systematically for sites where early hominids provide evidence for human origins and development. Their unwavering determination, thoroughness, use of new and untried dating techniques, public educational presentations, and scholarly publications have made Olduvai Gorge, the Laetoli footprints, and the australopithecines and other "early human" studies familiar to the American public.

While many of these approaches require exhaustive and wide-ranging, multidisciplinary research and correlation of data, the value of such painstaking research is clear. Flannery's meticulous investigations of plant and animal species exploitation by humankind in Mexico, at particular times and through time, have led to the formulation of a model for procurement patterns and seasonal "scheduling" of activities that permeates many of today's research projects (Flannery 1968, 74–75, and numerous other references), McNett (1971, 1985), McDowell (1972), Ritchie and Funk (1973), and Dent (1995).

Experimentation has become extremely important and enlightening in anthropological archaeology. Indeed, on occasion it has clarified major puzzles in the reconstruction of cultural behavior. Semenov's meticulous microscopic analysis of patterns of use and wear on lithic, bone, and wooden tools from museums and sites provided new insights into the techniques of manufacture and the nature of wear patterns on these objects (1964). Anna

Shepard (1956) and Fred Matson (1965) undertook parallel studies of ceramics to extract information about the makers and users of this medium. In many locations, archaeologists have buried sets of examples of material culture in distinctive environments to study *taphonomy*—the history of objects from initial burial to eventual recovery. These investigations serve several purposes. They may broaden insights into the behaviors, knowledge, and skills of the archaeologically known cultural groups. Or, they may verify that archaeological reconstructions and interpretations are accurate. They may prove that certain interpretations are incorrect by demonstrating that hypothesized techniques do not work as anticipated, perhaps enlightening researchers whose preconceived notions are wrong.

There are many other archaeologists who have contributed to our knowledge and who continue to revise our perspectives on the study of the human past. Some archaeologists are studying their own ancestry or heritage, as is common in Europe; others are studying the pasts of other cultures. In the Americas, for example, many archaeologists emphasize Native Americans, the "original" inhabitants of the Western Hemisphere. Today, this includes research by some of the descendants of these people, but the majority of researchers tend to be of European ancestry. In some instances, this generates resentment and suspicion among some groups of Native Americans who view their history as personal and private. The November/December 2000 issue of *Archaeology* contains an article by Joe Watkins, a Native American archaeologist (Watkins 2000, 36–41). An excerpt from his article reflects some of the conflicting responses and viewpoints. His experiences while trying to bridge two worlds demonstrate some examples of the difficulties encountered: "Because I was a Native American, my professors didn't think I could be an objective scientist, while American Indians distrusted my motives in studying archaeology.... I was told by one instructor that the only reason I was accepted at SMU was because I was Indian and had my own funding ... (Watkins 2000, 38)."

Fortunately, Watkins did not let these viewpoints discourage him, and completed his Ph.D. Following this accomplishment, he began to work for the Bureau of Indian Affairs in Oklahoma. He stated that in this capacity, he attempts to satisfy his employers and to demonstrate that what he does in his job benefits Native Americans as well as archaeology. He expressed concern that some archaeologists do not always keep in mind that the artifacts and sites they study are more than things. These archaeologists may need to remind themselves that the sites and objects represent people, their behavior, their beliefs, and their interactions and interrelationships with their environments. In his view, Native Americans do not lose sight of the importance of their interrelationships with their environments (Watkins 2000, 40).

Watkins pointed out that added to the suspicions of some archaeologists that a Native American archaeologist cannot be objective about Native American archaeological sites is the suspicion of some Native Americans that a professional archaeologist who is a Native American is a "sell-out" or a "Camp Indian." He noted that this might change if there were more than ten Native Americans with doctoral degrees in archaeology, and twenty with master's degrees (Watkins 2000, 40). In the meantime, Watkins urges archaeologists, Native Americans, and all people to work for greater tolerance of one another (Watkins 2000, 41).

When we say we are studying one another or are trying to be objective about what we study, we need to remember that we may be doing so within our own belief system and we may not be looking beyond ourselves and our own viewpoints. Judging others and their beliefs, technology, and behaviors as they would fit with our own is ethnocentrism. It is far more beneficial to our understanding of what people do and how they do it if we take a different approach. Attempting to view people and their behaviors, technology, and beliefs in a manner that may help us see more clearly what they believe and how they arrived at particular ways and means of doing what they do will demonstrate much more accurately how and why their behaviors differ from our own. This view is *cultural relativism*—trying to see others as they see themselves.

The bottom line of all of this may be that all of us need to try to transcend the so-called party lines—of, for example, professional archaeologist vs. Native American—to try to work out some kinds of compromises. While this is a tall order, it is the most useful approach to the complex differences of viewpoint found among human groups everywhere in the world.

Ethics and laws are a major concern in archaeology, as in all other aspects of our behavior as human beings. Much legislation has been written in an attempt to regulate archaeological research and to provide ethical guidelines and standards to protect the cultural heritage of those affected by such research. Providing these guidelines helps town planners, developers, and others who may be affected by them understand what is required by law and how these requirements are to be implemented. The National Register of Historic Places and the State Registers or Landmarks Registers were developed as the result of some of the legislation. The Secretary of the Interior has a special role as overseer and coordinator of the Federal Archeology Program in the United States. In 1998, at the request of the William M. Beauchamp Chapter of the New York State Archaeological Association, I drafted a summary of major archaeological legislation, with some emphasis on New York State. The purpose was to list the titles of the legislation so readers could gain access to the full documents if they wished. The U.S. Government Printing Office, the National Park Service, the Society for American Archaeology, and the Federal Register are sources of information. For state and local information, the state historic preservation offices (often referred to as SHPOs), state museums, colleges and universities, and local archaeological and historical societies are the best sources of local information.

The following is a brief list of federal legislation. First, came the Antiquities Act of 1906 (P. L. 59–209), enacted to protect archaeological sites on federal lands.

A series of revisions and expansions followed. These included the National Park Service Organization Act of 1916 (P. L. 64–235), the Historic Sites Act of 1935, the Federal Aid Highway Act of 1956 (P. L. 91–605), the Reservoir Salvage Act of 1960 (P. L. 86–523), the National Historic Preservation Act of 1966 (P. L. 95–515), amended in 1980 with codification of portions of Executive Order 11593, the Department of Transportation Act of 1966 (P. L. 89–670), the National Environmental Policy Act of 1969 (P. L. 91–190), Executive Order 11593, the 1971 "Protection and Enhancement of the Cultural Environment" (16 USC 470), the Archeological and Historic Preservation Act, 1974 (P. L. 93–291), the American Indian Religious Freedom Act, 1978 (P. L. 95–341), the Archaeological Resources Protection Act, 1979 (P. L. 96–95), supplementing the 1906 Antiquities Act, the Arctic Research Policy Act, 1984 (P. L. 98–373), and the Native American Graves Protection and Repatriation Act of 1990 (P. L. 101–601).

From this legislation have come requirements for archaeological studies (as part of the required Environmental Impact Statements) of lands or structures that are federal, state, or local properties that are to be developed or modified using government monies. The legislation has served as a protection for many (potentially) archaeologically sensitive areas. In his new book, Watkins (2000a) refers to the implementation of the laws, as well as the laws themselves.

Meanwhile, cases relating to the Native American Graves Protection and Repatriation Act of 1990 continue to be in the news. Syracuse Online (http://www.syracuse.com/news/index. ssf?/newsstories/city/20001206_rnbones.html) offers a report by Mike McAndrew entitled "Native Americans' Remains to Be Returned." Human skeletal remains of 241 Native Americans excavated from sites in Upstate New York, as well as 8,876 artifacts that have been classified as grave goods associated with these human remains, have been identified and documented as 200- to 450-year-old members of the Haudenosaunee (Iroquois Confederacy). "These are our ancestors," Chief Irving Powless stated. "We want them returned to where they belong—to Mother Earth."

Included are remains of 141 people from the Seneca Nation, 43 from the Mohawk Nation, 32 from the Cayuga Nation, and 25 from the Onondaga Nation. The Rochester Museum has carried out lengthy inventories of their stored and curated materials over the years since the 1990 legislation was passed. In the year 2000, the museum returned "skeletal remains of 25 Oneidas and 45 burial objects that were excavated from Oneida Nation grave sites in Stockbridge, Eaton and Verona," according to McAndrews.

Professional archaeologists, some avocational archaeologists, and some Native Americans agree that much scientific information about human behavior, illnesses, and biogenetic data may be gained from study of any human skeletal materials and their contexts. Much of this information may be unavailable from any other sources, and should broaden and enrich what is known from oral tradition.

On the other hand, many Native American advocates for the immediate return of all Native American human remains believe museums and archaeologists should apologize for all past excavations of Native Americans. In their view, such activity reflected the way in which Native Americans were considered objects of curiosity, to be pillaged and dehumanized by those who studied them. Many archaeologists counter that they valued the people they studied and tried to record as much and as many kinds of information about them as they could. Further, they argue that what they have done and the manner in which they have done it is respectful and humanitarian, and should not be confused or equated with the activities of looters. Those who dig up graves for the express purpose of finding objects for private collections and for sale for profit are not the same as archaeologists or reputable museums or other institutions where the study of human beings and their diversity is valued.

Museums throughout the United States are searching their collections and consulting with Native American groups about the materials that must be returned, as required under NAGPRA. Some Native American spokespersons have requested apologies from organizations who are returning the human remains and artifacts that have been judged to be sacred by these nations. In an Upstate New York case, Connie Bodner, director of collections and research at Rochester Museum provided an archaeological viewpoint that was supported by the Rochester Museum. She described the manner in which these remains were acquired by them, when they were received, how they were treated when they arrived at the museum, and what museum personnel at that time perceived to be appropriate for such donations. Sources of collections included expeditions from 1920 to 1950, purchases from local private collectors, gifts from various sources, and materials gathered when public-works crews unearthed them during construction projects. Once in the museum, these materials were stored safely and carefully. This prevented their destruction, resale, or dispersal at the hands of souvenir-hunters. Bodner stated that the viewpoint presented officially by the Rochester Museum is that the museum's policy was respectful and careful. The museum does not apologize for their well-intended actions.

ARCHAEOLOGY EDUCATION TODAY

The Society for American Archaeology (SAA) has published a book entitled *Teaching Archaeology in the Twenty-First Century*, edited by Susan J. Bender and George S. Smith (2000). Topics in it include what archaeology is, what its importance and significance are in the "real world," how it contributes to this same real world, and what its priorities are or should be. The curriculum devised to prepare archaeologists for today's situations requires revision and updating, according to Bender and Smith. There should be more emphasis on NAGPRA and other state and federal legislation as well as on reasons why the legislation has developed as it has. Students and the general public need to be shown more clearly and reasonably why archaeological resources need to be studied and why sensitivity to, and acceptance of, the beliefs of descendants of those who are studied should be emphasized. Indeed, students should be trained to understand the perspective of those whose ancestors they study. Since these students will be the next professional archaeologists, it is vital that the curriculum provide techniques for conveying to the public not only the students' respect and sensitivity for those they study but their justification for doing archaeology.

David G. Anderson's article, "Archaeologists as Anthropologists: The Question of Training," perceives little change in the way anthropology departments train their students. Since many individuals in these programs plan to work in nonacademic settings, some believe that "what is taught in the four traditional subfields (*including archaeology*), has little or no utility to the practice of archaeology today. Indeed, some believe that much of the subject matter of anthropology is "trivial, arcane, or otherwise irrelevant to many practicing archaeologists" (Anderson in Bender and Smith 2000, 141–146). Anderson also notes the following:

> The counter-argument, that anthropology is relevant in archaeological training, has been ... expressed by Kent Flannery (1982), in his classic "Golden Marshalltown" article. In this paper, Flannery argued that the concept of culture (encompassing all four subfields) was an essential unifying framework for scholars responsible for finding, documenting, and interpreting the remains left behind by past cultural systems, and produced by a wide range of behaviors. Anthropology teaches a holistic view of human behavior, and some exposure to the discipline is probably essential to the training of an effective archaeologist. You can indeed find employment in archaeology without any training in anthropology, but you can do archaeology better if you have been educated within an anthropological framework. (Anderson in Bender and Smith 2000, 141–142)

It appears that Anderson would like to revise curriculum so that students could take courses in the four subfields of anthropology that are courses with an archaeological slant, for instance "Linguistics for Archaeologists," just as McGimsey suggested in 1994. [Note: The writer took a course of that type in 1971, as a candidate for a Ph.D. in anthropology. It provided insights that were valuable, at that level of training, but would have been less informative without previous courses devoted to each subdiscipline individually.]

Anderson offers another suggestion that would appeal to many students, although one could argue strongly against it. He believes that if a graduate anthropology student sees the need for a particular foreign language, he or she will learn it and should not be required to take it as a degree qualification. In his view, "the elimination of the language requirement at the master's level might free up time for more archaeology courses. In addition, specific courses that could be offered to archaeologists could include preservation law and management, GIS/computer applications, statistical analyses/quantitative methods, business management skills, and technical writing. Likewise, archaeological ethics must receive a high priority, with an emphasis on our obligations to the archaeological record, to reporting our findings responsibly, and to our subjects and audience, including the descendants of the peoples under study" (Anderson in Bender and Smith 2000, 142).

WHOSE ARCHAEOLOGY IS IT?

Throughout *Archaeology: Introductory Guide for Classroom and Field*, the emphasis has been on methodology and explanations of it, although there were allusions to the nonarchaeological people with whom you will interact—site visitors, friends, and others who might inquire about what you were doing. Possibly, there should be stress placed on the domain of archaeology. To whom does archaeology belong?

Some Native Americans have claimed that nonnative archaeologists do their researches on Native Americans and publish their work, but fail to share what they have learned with the descendants of those studied. Perhaps this is a shortcoming that could be improved quite easily. Gestures such as invitations to Native Americans to visit archaeological sites that are in regions where they have traditional lands, offers to provide talks and copies of reports, and encouragement of Native American students and their families to ask questions and participate in the research may have been neglected, in some cases. Increasingly, there are archaeological programs in which there are Native American participants, just as there have been more occasions when African American participants have been encouraged to take part in studies of sites in the Southeast and in New York City's historic African-American burying ground site. Study of human beings of every time and place is important to everyone, and "belongs" to all of us, in my view.

Charles R. McGimsey III and Hester A. Davis (in Bender and Smith 2000, 5–8), argue convincingly that archaeological training must underscore the direct connections between the study of the human past and today's human beings! Bluntly stated: "Public archaeology … entails the effective coordination, encouragement, and integration of all who wish to participate in, contribute to, and benefit from all aspects of archaeological work. Only insofar as archaeology becomes effective public archaeology can the creation and maintenance of appropriate public attitudes occur, which in turn permits decision makers (or cultural resource managers, among others) to develop and apply the legal and administrative mechanisms and the funding necessary for participants in archaeology of all persuasions to work effectively together to achieve archaeology's three basic goals: (1) maximum conservation of the archaeological resource base, (2) derivation of the maximum amount of information from that base, and (3) communication of the results of that conservation and research to the largest possible public audience."

Peter N. Peregrine (2001) makes similar points while emphasizing some that are not as evident in McGimsey and Davis' article. He notes that we do archaeology "to recognize the contributions and achievements of our predecessors," to help us understand the origins in the past of many of the things we do today, to help us avoid the repetition of mistakes made in the past, and to reconstruct and revise our reconstructions of past human behavior as new information and insights become available (Peregrine 2001, xiii–xviii). It is not until Chapter 13 of Peregrine's book that laws and ethics are highlighted, although buried in Chapter 12, "Presenting Results," is reference to "grey literature." Peregrine defines this as "archaeological reports with limited distribution and no peer review. These are often 'contract' reports, written to describe the results of archaeological salvage work, but they also include some research reports produced by university or museum departments and even survey and excavation reports produced by amateur societies" (Peregrine 2001, 203). Although these reports tend to be read more widely by a general readership, it appears that Peregrine views them as both mixed in quality and of less value as a product of archaeology. This may be the case for the professional archaeological community where there is a modicum of ease in reading the peer-reviewed professional journal offerings, doctoral dissertations, books and monographs. However, perhaps a broader range of people will read all or parts of the so-called "grey literature." Since archaeology depends on the continued interest and support of the general public to survive, perhaps closer scrutiny of what goes into the "grey literature" would be wise and informative, and maybe it is necessary. After all, students, avocational archaeologists, and professional archaeologists are only a small proportion of the overall human population. Archaeology is not just about a small segment, but about all of the human past—and it is done by archaeologists for everyone—not just for some exclusive inner circle. As McGimsey and Davis put it, "There is no such thing as 'private archaeology'" (McGimsey 1972, 5, in Bender and Smith 2000, 5).

Ethics are an extremely important aspect of one's view of the world and one's behavior as a result of this view. Each society has sets of culturally defined "right" or "correct" ways to behave. Often, these ways have a moral connotation and imply a range of meanings, some legal, some traditional, and some religious in nature. Often, we assume that our ethics are shared by all in our society and frequently, we are surprised to encounter contradictions to this expectation. The ethics in anthropological archaeology have developed out of the changing perspectives found within the discipline itself and the directions its research and researchers have taken. Others have resulted from the changing perceptions we have of what environment can tell about human activities of the past and present and how past archaeologists may have viewed their context. The sociopolitical climate of today stresses greater sensitivity to diverse viewpoints about the nature of human heritage, especially as it relates to human physical remains. In some cases, there may be irreconcilable differences in outlooks toward what is or is not ethical behavior in the case of research. Evaluating the ways in which archaeologists and other people deal with these differences of perspective may give clues to changes in other aspects of today's interpersonal relationships, and may give hints of how lessons of the past have impact on the present.

In the bibliography, there are several examples that illustrate some of the ethical issues. Among these are books by Ernestene Green (1984), Charles R. McGimsey, III (1972), Clement Meighan (1986), and the Quarterly Federal Archeology Report published by the National Park Service (U.S. Department of the Interior). The Society for American Archaeology and various bulletins from state archaeological associations are other sources of data on ethics in archaeology.

A recently reorganized and broadened professional organization for archaeologists is the Register of Professional Archaeologists (RPA). Within its first edition are data on archaeological ethics, its membership-ratified "Code of Conduct, Standards of Research Performance, Guidelines and Standards for Archaeological Field School," and listings of State and Tribal historic preservation officers and deputies, as well as a listing of its membership (RPA 2000–2001). The thorough coverage reflects the concerns of the membership.

SUMMARY AND CONCLUSIONS

It is an exciting time for archaeology. More and more new ideas for the study of the past are developing, new and diverse connections between people from all over the world are generating the exchange of viewpoints, discoveries, and suggestions. Increasingly, there are members of groups previously studied only by outsiders who are participating in the studies of their own heritage. This has been the case in Connecticut, for example, where the Mashantuket Pequot Museum and Research Center hired a team of archaeologists to provide on-site information and assistance with their museum project, including numerous Native American participants. Research on the Oneida Nation's lands in central New York has been undertaken jointly with archaeologists from Colgate University and personnel from the Oneida Nation. This is a similar effort in which Haudenosaunee (Oneida) students are learning archaeological techniques while studying their own ancestors, and are incorporating data from consultation with their elders for greater understanding of their heritage and oral tradition. The Navajo and Hopi nations have devised archaeological teams to help protect their archaeologically known resources, and the Haida have worked with archaeologists to uncover, study, and protect an entire village in Washington State, where a mudslide had buried one of their prehistoric villages. The resultant Haida-run museum, videotapes, and other publications have been extremely informative.

The NOVA videotape, "Mystery of the First Americans," released in 2000, illustrates another aspect of this cooperative venture. In coastal Alaska where Ice Age archaeological sites have been found in deep caves along the seacoast, local Native Americans have participated in the archaeological exploration of the sites. Their oral tradition indicates that they have lived in that region for many generations, and their maritime adaptation included the exploitation of foods harvested from the sea. When human remains were discovered in the depths of one of the so-called "bear caves," and analysis of the dentition of the individual found revealed he had a diet based on sea foods, the sense of continuity of today's people's presence in the area pleased and satisfied them. Although they had not doubted their oral traditions, the archaeological finds, in their view, validated their beliefs for "outsiders" to see.

There are other examples of this kind of cooperative venture for reconstructing parts of the cultural heritage of all of us. Some are reported in National Park Service publications; others are featured in local newspapers. Certainly, the cooperation of those whose cultural heritage may be represented is most beneficial. Ideally, the direction of some of these projects will be in the hands of those individuals increasingly, as they acquire the training that will complement their insights and basic knowledge of their heritage.

The Internet offers enormous variety and opportunity for gathering information. Although the data must be screened carefully and evaluated for validity, there are many reputable sources for garnering newly released information, with illustrations, almost at the moment when these discoveries have been made. More and more colleges, universities, museums, and journals are offering publications on-line and clever archaeological simulations for public use.

Web sites abound, with ever-increasing arrays of links to a variety of topics. Many of the anthropological sites include links to specialists or frequently updated lists of programs, field schools, and tours. Opportunities to ask questions and get prompt answers are another luxury provided on many of the web sites. It has been encouraging to see that at least some Native American nations have archaeological links attached to their web sites. Perhaps this is a first step in improving the interrelationships between archaeologists who study Native Americans and the descendants of those they study.

Archaeology reflects the society in which it is found. In the past, its participants have made mistakes that some may regret today. Debates have raged, and continue to do so, over who should or should not have access to some kinds of archaeological information. This is true in particular as it relates to the Native American Graves Protection and Repatriation Act. I believe there are many other aspects of the story of the human past and the remarkable things that human beings have accomplished, developed, and learned, that archaeology is helping to reconstruct for all to admire.

We should continue to work together—professional, student, and avocational archaeologist, as well as Native Americans and the rest of the public—to find common ground, rather than becoming bogged down in points of disagreement. This is part of what it means when we say that archaeology belongs to everyone.

APPENDIX

ARCHAEOLOGICAL FORMS

ON THE FOLLOWING PAGES, THIS APPENDIX PROVIDES EXAMPLES OF FORMS FOR recording various features. Bear in mind that often the researcher has to add other categories of information to the forms to fit the particular feature. Archaeological forms tend to be guidelines, not the last word in record-keeping.

Note that the forms represent state, county, and river survey varieties. They include examples spanning thirty years of experimentation and elaboration. Because some types of forms have been standardized for use by professional archaeologists, state historic preservation administrators, avocational archaeologists, or anyone else within a state who might happen to be reporting discovery of a site, the first three examples—New York State Prehistoric Archaeological Site Inventory Form (pages 130–131), New York State Historic Archaeological Site Inventory Form (pages 132–134), and New York State Building/Structure Inventory Form (pages 135–138)—are used currently in New York State. For comparison, two forms from Virginia follow (pages 139–141). Since river valley surveys tend to include more than one state, examples from the D.C. Consortium of Universities Potomac River Valley Archaeological Survey are included (pages 142–143). To complete the sample, there are Cortland County, New York survey examples, including level report (page 144), two alternative forms for stratigraphic profiles and plan views (floor plans) (pages 145–146), feature record (page 147), and artifact inventory sheet (pages 148–149). A sample level report form of an excavation unit recorded in 1996 (page 150) and an artifact inventory sheet from 1997 (page 151) complete the set. The Cortland County examples are used for site reporting and supplement those provided to the New York State Division for Historic Preservation and the New York State Museum for their files. Finally, pages 152–153 contain a brief description of methods for determining soil acidity and reasons for determining this.

NEW YORK STATE PREHISTORIC ARCHAEOLOGICAL SITE INVENTORY FORM

For Office Use Only—Site Identifier _____

Project Identifier _____ Date _____

Your Name _____ Phone _____

Address _____

_____

_____ Zip _____

Organization (if any) _____

1. Site Identifier(s)_____

2. County _____ One of following:

   City _____

   Township _____

   Incorporated Village _____

   Unincorporated Village

   or Hamlet _____

3. Present Owner _____

   Address _____

   _____ Zip _____

4. Site Description (check all appropriate categories):

   __ Stray find   __ Cave/Rock shelter
   __ Workshop   __ Pictograph
   __ Quarry   __ Mound
   __ Burial   __ Shell midden
   __ Village   __ Surface evidence
   __ Camp   __ Material in plow zone
   __ Material below plow zone   __ Buried evidence
   __ Intact occupation floor   __ Single component
   __ Evidence of features   __ Stratified
   __ Multi component

   Location:

   __ Under cultivation   __ Never cultivated
   __ Previously cultivated   __ Pastureland
   __ Woodland   __ Flood plain
   __ Upland   __ Sustaining erosion

   Soil Drainage:

   __ Excellent   __ Good
   __ Fair   __ Poor

Slope:

__ Flat   __ Gentle

__ Moderate   __ Steep

Distance to nearest water from site (approx.) _____

Elevation _____

5. Site Investigation (append additional sheets, if necessary):

Surface   __ Date(s) _____

               __ Site Map (Submit with form*)

               __ Collection

Subsurface   __ Date(s) _____

    Testing:

      __ Shovel   __ Coring

      __ Other _____ Unit size _____

       No. of units _____ (Submit plan of units with form*)

Excavation:

    Unit size _____ No. of units _____

    (Submit plan of units with form*)

    *Submission should be 8½ x 11 inches, if feasible.

Investigator _____

Manuscript or published report(s) (reference fully) _____

_____

Present repository of materials _____

_____

6. Component(s) (cultural affiliation/dates) _____

_____

7. List of material remains (be as specific as possible in identifying object and material)_____

_____

    __ If historic materials are evident, check here and fill out historic site form.

8. Map References: Map or maps showing exact location and extent of site must accompany this form and must be identified by source and date. Keep this submission to 8½ x 11 inches, if possible.

USGS 7½ Minute Series Quad   Name _____

For Office Use Only _____ UTM Coordinates _____

9. Photography (optional for environmental impact survey)

Please submit 5 x 7 inch black and white print(s) showing the current state of the site. Provide a label for the print(s) on a separate sheet.

NEW YORK STATE HISTORIC ARCHAEOLOGICAL SITE INVENTORY FORM

For Office Use Only—Site Identifier _____

Project Identifier _____ Date _____

Your Name_____ Phone _____

Address _____

_____

_____ Zip _____

Organization (if any) _____

1. Site Identifier(s) _____

2. County _____   One of following:

                                City _____

                          /   Township _____

                                Incorporated Village _____

                    /   Unincorporated Village

                                or Hamlet _____

3. Present Owner _____

    Address _____

    _____ Zip _____

4. Site Description (check all appropriate categories):

    Structure/Site

    Superstructure:

    __ Complete   __ Partial

    __ Collapsed   __ Not evident

    Foundation:

    __ Above ground level   __ Below ground level

    __ Not evident

    Structural subdivisions apparent _____

    Only surface traces visible _____

    Buried traces detected _____

    List construction materials (be as specific as possible) _____

    _____

    _____

    Grounds:

    __ Under cultivation   __ Sustaining erosion

    __ Woodland   __ Upland

    __ Never cultivated   __ Previously cultivated

    __ Flood plain   __ Pastureland

Slope:

__ Flat   __ Gentle

__ Moderate   __ Steep

Distance to nearest water from structure (approx.) _____

Elevation _____

5.   Site Investigation (append additional sheets, if necessary):

Surface   __ Date(s) _____

                  __ Site Map (Submit with form*)

                  __ Collection

Subsurface   __ Date(s) _____

    Testing:

      __ Shovel   __ Coring

      __ Other _____ Unit size _____

      No. of units _____ (Submit plan of units with form*)

Excavation:

    Unit size _____ No. of units _____

    (Submit plan of units with form*)

    *Submission should be 8½ x 11 inches, if feasible.

Investigator _____

Manuscript or published report(s) (reference fully) _____

_____

Present repository of materials _____

_____

6.   Site inventory:

a. Date constructed or occupation period _____

b. Previous owners, if known _____

c. Modifications, if known _____

_____

    (Append additional sheets, if necessary)

7.   Site documentation (append additional sheets, if necessary):

a. Historic map references

    (1)Name _____ Date _____

      Source _____

      Present location of original, if known _____

    (2)Name _____ Date _____

      Source _____

      Present location of original, if known _____

b. Representation in existing photography
  (1)Photo date _____ Where located _____
  (2)Photo date _____ Where located _____
c. Primary and secondary source documentation (reference fully)

_____

_____

d. Persons with memory of site:
  (1)Name _____ Address _____
  (2)Name _____ Address _____

8. List of material remains other than those used in construction (be as specific as possible in identifying object and material):

_____

_____

___ If prehistoric materials are evident, check here and fill out historic site form.

9. Map References: Map or maps showing exact location and extent of site must accompany this form and must be identified by source and date. Keep this submission to 8½ x 11 inches, if possible.

USGS 7½ Minute Series Quad   Name _____

For Office Use Only _____ UTM Coordinates _____

10. Photography (optional for environmental impact survey)

Please submit 5 x 7 inch black and white print(s) showing the current state of the site. Provide a label for the print(s) on a separate sheet.

NEW YORK STATE BUILDING/STRUCTURE INVENTORY FORM

For Office Use Only—Site Identifier _____

Your Name _____

Unique Site No. _____

Quad Name _____

Neg. # _____

Your Address _____ Date _____

_____ Phone _____

Organization (if any) _____

IDENTIFICATION

1. Building Name(s) _____

   _____

2. County _____

3. Street Location _____

4. Ownership   a. Public _____   b. Private _____

5. Present Owner _____

   Address _____

6. Use   Original _____

   _____

   Present _____

7. Accessibility: Exterior visible from public road   yes ____   no____

   To Public : Interior accessible

   Explain _____

   _____

DESCRIPTION

8. Building Material:

   a. Clapboard____   b. Stone   ____

   c. Brick____   d. Board & batten ____

   e. Cobblestone ____   f. Shingle ____

   g. Stucco ____   h. Metal siding ____

   i. Composition material ____ j. Other ____

9. Structural System (if known):

    a. Wood frame with interlocking joints ____

    b. Wood frame with light members____

    c. Masonry load bearing walls ____

    d. Metal (explain) _____

    e. Other _____

    f. Solid log ____

    <u>Foundation</u>

    g. Fieldstone   Dry ____   Mortared ____

    <u>Construction</u>

    h. Cut stone   Dry ____   Mortared ____

    i. Brick____

    j. Metal ____

    k. Fabricated____

    l. Poured concrete____   Block ____

    m. None ____

10. Condition:

    a. Excellent ____

    b. Good ____

    c. Fair ____

    d. Deteriorated ____

11. Integrity:

    a. Original site _____

    b. Moved—if so, when _____

    c. List major alteration(s) and dates (if known) _____

    _____

    _____

12. Photo (attach)

13. Map (attach)

14. Threats to Building:

    a. None known ____

    b. Zoning ____

    c. Roads ____

    d. Developers ____

    e. Deterioration____

    f. Other _____

15. Related Outbuildings and Property:
     a. Barn _____
     b. Carriage house _____
     c. Garage _____
     d. Privy   _____   .
     e Shed _____
     f. Greenhouse _____
     g. Shop_____
     h. Gardens _____
     i. Landscape features _____
     j. Other _____
     k. Well _____   l. Fence/wall _____
16. Surroundings of Building (check more than one if necessary):
     a. Open land_____
     b. Woodland _____
     c. Scattered buildings _____
     d. Densely built up _____
     e. Commercial _____
     f. Industrial _____
     g. Residential _____
     h. Other _____
17. Interrelationship of Building and Surroundings (indicate if building or structure is in an historic district)

     _____

     _____

18. Other Notable Features of Building and Site (including interior features if known)

     _____

     _____

SIGNIFICANCE

19. Date of Initial Construction _____
     Earliest Map Showing This Building _____
     Name _____
     Date _____
     Architect _____

Builder _____

Were Earlier Maps Available?   Yes ____   No ____

20. Historical and Architectural Importance _____

_____

_____

_____

_____

21. Sources _____

_____

_____

_____

_____

22. Theme _____

_____

_____

_____

_____

COMMONWEALTH OF VIRGINIA
VIRGINIA STATE LIBRARY
ARCHAEOLOGICAL SURVEY SITE RECORD

County _____   Site Number _____

Map Reference _____   Date Recorded _____

Descriptive Location _____

_____

_____

Owner and Address _____

Attitude toward Excavation_____

Previous Owners _____

Tenant _____

Informants_____

Previous Name of Site_____

Dimensions of Site _____

Depth of Site _____

Character of Soil_____

Nearest Water Source _____

General Surroundings_____

_____

_____

Present Condition _____

_____

_____

Previous Excavations _____

_____

_____

Surface Materials Collected _____

_____

_____

Surface Material Reported _____

_____

_____

Owner of Material _____

Remarks _____

_____

_____

_____

_____

Recommendations for Further Work_____

_____

_____

_____

_____

Photographed _____

Mapped _____

Recorded by _____

COMMONWEALTH OF VIRGINIA
VIRGINIA STATE LIBRARY
ARCHAEOLOGICAL SURVEY SITE RECORD MAP

Site No. _____   County _____

Location _____

Mapped by _____   Date _____

A	B	C	D	E	F	G

REMARKS   Scale: Each Space = _____ Feet

D.C. CONSORTIUM OF UNIVERSITIES
POTOMAC RIVER VALLEY ARCHAEOLOGICAL SURVEY
ECOLOGICAL INFORMATION

Site _____

Vegetation _____

_____

_____

Fauna _____

_____

_____

Soil _____

    Type and Sample No. _____

Physiographic Zone _____

_____

_____

Ecological Features:

    Nearest Water _____

    Quarries _____

_____

    Ponds _____

_____

    Marsh _____

_____

    Other Features _____

_____

_____

_____

Remarks _____

_____

_____

_____

_____

Recorded by _____ Date _____

D.C. CONSORTIUM OF UNIVERSITIES
POTOMAC RIVER VALLEY ARCHAEOLOGICAL SURVEY
DAILY FIELD NOTES IN ARCHAEOLOGY

Name _____

Date _____

Site _____

Units worked in _____

Level: from _____   to _____

Other Work: Mapping, Photography, Survey, Catalog (give details)

_____

_____

_____

_____

Features Worked on (use reverse side for diagram)

Burials Worked on (use reverse side for diagram)

Stratigraphy Noted_____

_____

_____

_____

Summary of Artifacts (draw unusual pieces)

_____

_____

_____

_____

Give your own ideas of how the over-all cultural interpretation was added to or
changed by what you found today _____

_____

_____

_____

_____

CORTLAND COUNTY, NEW YORK
ARCHAEOLOGICAL SURVEY LEVEL REPORT

Site _____

Square/Unit _____

Level_____ · _____

Date Level Started _____ Date Level Finished _____

Depth to Floor at _____ Corner (Square/Master Datum Stake) _____ B.D.

Screened? _____ Screen Mesh Size _____

Floor Troweled, Checked for Features? _____

Walls Troweled, Checked for Features? _____

Features Present or Indicated _____

_____

Nature of Soil_____

Soil Sample Taken _____

Sample Numbers _____

Artifacts Recovered _____

_____

_____

_____

Artifact Bag Numbers _____

_____

_____

Debris Recovered Other Than Artifacts _____

_____

_____

_____

Floor Plan Drawn on Graphed Sheet on Reverse? _____

Remarks (Photographs? Drawings? Other?) _____

_____

_____

_____

Recorded by _____

Supervisor's Approval _____

Date _____

CORTLAND COUNTY, NEW YORK
ARCHAEOLOGICAL SITE SURVEY STRATIGRAPHIC PROFILE SHEET

Site _____   Date _____

Block (Square) _____   Depth to Floor _____

Profile of (which?) _____ Wall   Stakes in Corners _____

Scale _____   Key to Features _____

Recorded by _____

Comments _____

_____

_____

CORTLAND COUNTY, NEW YORK
ARCHAEOLOGICAL SURVEY FORMS
WALL PROFILE OR PLAN VIEW OF FLOOR OF EXCAVATION

Site _____ Excavation Unit _____ Date _____

Floor Plan/Wall Profile (circle one)

Orientation _____

Label corners of diagram (for floor plan, North = top of page)

(for wall profile, label upper left, ex. NE and right ex. NW corners of diagram for North Wall Profile)

Scale: Each square = .5 foot

Recorders _____

Supervisor's Approval _____

CORTLAND COUNTY, NEW YORK
ARCHAEOLOGICAL SITE SURVEY FEATURE RECORD

Site _____   Block or Square(s) _____

Provenience _____   Horizontal Location _____

Depth Below (Square/Master) Datum _____

Feature Number _____

Feature Definition _____

_____

_____

_____

Associated Artifacts and Debris _____

Feature Dimensions _____

Stratigraphy Noted _____

_____

_____

_____

_____

Comments _____

_____

_____

_____

_____

Drawings (Graphed?) _____   Photographic Numbers _____

                     _____   _____

                     _____   _____

                     _____   _____

                     _____   _____

                     _____   _____

Exposed by _____   Recorded by _____

Date _____

Supervisor's Approval _____

CORTLAND COUNTY, NEW YORK
ARCHAEOLOGICAL SURVEY ARTIFACT INVENTORY SHEET

Site _____   Square Block _____

Level_____   B.D. _____

Artifactual Materials in This Square/Block and Level:

Points (Number) _____   Material (Itemize) _____

_____

_____

_____

Comments _____

_____

_____

_____

Flakes/Debitage (Number) _____   Material (Itemize) _____

_____

_____

_____

Comments (Utilized? Worked? Shatter?) _____

_____

_____

_____

Pottery (Number/Itemize) _____

_____

_____

Decorated? _____

Comments _____

_____

_____

_____

Cores (Number)_____   Material (Itemize) _____

_____

_____

_____

Choppers (Number) _____ Material (Itemize) _____

_____

_____

_____

Scrapers, Awls, etc._____ Material (Itemize) _____

_____

_____

_____

Comments _____

_____

_____

Miscellaneous Finds (Give Number, Material, and Other Identifiable Characteristics) _____

_____

_____

_____

Recorded by _____

Supervisor's Approval _____

Date _____

35 CO 30
1996 LEVEL REPORT

Unit/Soil pH	Level	Nature of Soil	Artifacts
N200E35 PH 5.7/6.7	0-1.0' B.D.	silty, med. dark brown gravel, roots, plowzone	*91 FCR, 10 chert flakes, 1 abrader, 13 coal pieces, 1 sandstone hammer-stone
PH 6.7	1.0-1.5' B.D.	loamy dark brown silt gravel	5 chert flakes, 1 burned chopper, 1 burned gouge, 2 cinders, 4 coal fragments, 24 wood charcoal fragments, 2 burned abraders, 1 hammer-stone, *126 FCR
PH 6.0	1.5-1.7' B.D.	silty, med. gray-yellow (Southeast rock cluster)	1 rusty nail, 1 chert fragment, 13 wood charcoal, *26 FCR,
(Rain slump)		wet, silty gray-yellow	*9 FCR, 1 wood charcoal
PH 6.5 (S.W. end)	1.5-2.0' B.D.	silty, gray, gravelly	*29 FCR, 5 chert flakes, 1 netsinker, 1 nutting stone, 1 flat stone chopper
Sondage	2.0-3.0' B.D.	silty-to-gritty sand, gray	*15 FCR, 2 hammer-stones
PH 6.9		large, flat boulder at base	(2.0-2.5' B.D.)

[Crew: Regina Rizzi, Jeffrey Plochocki 6/25–7/9/96]

35 CO 30

1997 ARTIFACT INVENTORY

Excavation Unit	Date	Location/Level	Artifacts
S100 W195	7/14/97	Southwest Feature	charred fragments
S100 W195	7/15/97	Southwest Feature	44 charred wood fragments
S100 W195	7/7/97	1.0'–1.5' B.D.	1 nutting stone

ANALYSIS OF SOIL ACIDITY (PH) FOR ARCHAEOLOGY

Cornwall, I. W.
  1958 *Soils for the Archaeologist*. London: Phoenix House.
Cornwall, I. W.
  1963 "Soil-Science Helps the Archaeologist." In E. Pyddoke, ed., *The Scientist and Archaeology*. London: Phoenix House.
Deetz, J. and Dethlefsen, E.
  1963 "Soil pH as a Tool in Archaeological Site Interpretation." *American Antiquity* 20 (2): 242–243.
Jackson, M. L.
  1958 *Soil Chemical Analysis*. New York: Prentice Hall.

Soil pH stratification (or profiles/levels) is a valuable tool for interpretation of changes in land usage. The purpose of this process is to detect nonvisible stratigraphic differences in the apparently homogeneous or unstratified midden profiles in an archeological context. Further, investigations show that bone will not be preserved in soil with a pH value of 7.0 (neutral); values over 7.0 indicate a basic or alkaline medium; those below 7.0 are acid (Cornwall 1958).

Procedure: Determine soil pH at 1 ft. vertical and horizontal units over the entire vertical face of an excavation. Deetz and Dethlefsen (1963) utilized 20 ft. squares 5.5 ft. deep for their sampling.

Method:
1. Take 100 cc of soil with a trowel and place it in a cardboard box (-es) for laboratory analysis
2. Divide each sample into 3 portions for separate testing.
3. Employ the "water saturation percentage method" (Jackson 1958)
   a. Take 3 separate 30–40 cc samples—place each in a 50 cc beaker and add distilled water in small increments from a wash bottle without stirring (to avoid puddling of soil and water) until samples are thoroughly wetted. Add a few more drops of water to make surface appear liquid.
   b. Stir mixture with a glass rod, adding water until suspension is of such a consistency that removal of the glass rod leaves a hole that closes slowly.
   c. Immediately insert the small electrodes of a Beckman Model 96 pH meter and record readings.

d. Repeat the procedure for each sample on different days (not vital if they correspond closely +/− .005 pH agreement). Use the mean of the 3 readings (from each sample at the site) to construct the pH profile.

Note: Today, there are a number of devices for use in the field that measure soil pH with some degree of accuracy. However, some chemical testing kits available today (2000–2001) offer greater accuracy and do not require the pH meter referred to above.

BIBLIOGRAPHY

Alland, A., Jr.
    1967   *Evolution and Human Behavior*. Garden City: Natural History Press.
American Geological Institute
    1976   *Dictionary of Geological Terms*. Rev. ed. Garden City: Doubleday Anchor Publications.
Aveni, A. F., ed.
    2000   *Annual Editions in Archaeology*. Sluice Dock, Guilford: Dushkin/McGraw-Hill.
Bender, S. J., and G. S. Smith, eds.
    2000   *Teaching Archaeology in the Twenty-First Century*. Washington, D.C.: The Society for American Archaeology.
Binford, L.
    1970   "Archaeology at Hatchery West." Memoir 24. Washington, D.C.: The Society for American Archaeology.
Binford, L., and S. Binford, eds.
    1968   *New Perspectives in Archeology*. Chicago: Aldine Publishing Company.
Bordaz, J.
    1968   *Tools of the Old Stone Age*. Garden City: Natural History Press.
Bordes, F.
    1968   *The Old Stone Age*. Garden City: Natural History Press.
Caldwell, J.
    1958   "Trend and Tradition in American Archeology." Memoir. Washington, D.C.: American Anthropological Association.
Callahan, E., ed.
    1974   "The Ape #3: Experimental Archeology Papers." Richmond: Virginia Commonwealth University.

Clarke, D.
1968   *Analytical Archeology*. London: Methuen Press.
Chang, K.
1967   "Major Aspects of the Interrelationship of Archaeology and Ethnology." *Current Anthropology* 8, no. 3: 227–243.
Cornwall, I. W.
1958   *Soils for the Archaeologist*. London: Phoenix House.
1963   "Soil-Science Helps the Archaeologist." In *The Scientist and Archaeology*. Ed. E. Pyddoke. London: Phoenix House.
Crabtree, D. E.
1972   "An Introduction to Flint-Working." Occasional papers of Idaho State University Museum 22. Pocatello, ID: Idaho State University.
Deetz, J.
1967   *Invitation to Archaeology*. Garden City: The Natural History Press.
Deetz, J., and E. Dethlefsen
1963   "Soil pH as a Tool in Archaeological Site Interpretation." *American Antiquity* 20, no. 2: 242–243.
Dent, R. J., Jr.
1995   *Chesapeake Prehistory: Old Traditions New Directions*. New York: Plenum Press.
Fagan, B. M.
1997   *In the Beginning: An Introduction to Archaeology*. 9th ed. New York: Addison Wesley Longman.
1999   *Archaeology: A Brief Introduction*. 7th ed. Upper Saddle River, NJ: Prentice Hall.
1999   *World Prehistory: A Brief Introduction*. 4th ed. New York: Addison Wesley Longman.
Fagan, B. M., and F. Van Noten
1971   *The Hunter-Gatherers of Gwisho*. Tervuren, Belgium: Musée Royal de l'Afrique Centrale.
Flannery, K.
1968   "Archaeological Systems Theory and Early Mesoamerica." In *Anthropological Archeology in the Americas*. Ed. B. Meggers. Washington, D.C.: The Anthropological Society of Washington.
Gardner, W. M., and C. W. McNett, Jr.
1970   "The Rowe Site." *Maryland Archaeology* 6: 1–29.
Go, K.
n.d.   "Out of ASU, into Africa: Prof, Team to Study Fossils." *The Arizona Republic*, on-line at <www.azcentral.com/community/comstories/0615fossils.shtml>.
Green, E. L., ed.
1984   *Ethics and Values in Archaeology*. New York: The Free Press.

Gross, J. I.
   1974   "Thunderbird Site Lithic Distributions." In *Flint Run Paleoindian
           Complex: A Preliminary Report 1971–73*. Ed. W. M. Gardner. Wash-
           ington, D.C.: Occasional Publication No. 1: Archaeology Labora-
           tory, Catholic University.
Haas, M.
   1965   "Other Culture vs. Own Culture: Some thoughts on L. White's
           Query." *American Anthropologist* 67: 1556–1560.
Harris, M.
   1968   "Comments: 359–361." In *New Perspectives in Archaeology*. Eds. L.
           Binford and S. Binford. Chicago: Aldine Publishing Company.
Hasten, L.
   2001   *Annual Editions: Archaeology 00/01*. Guilford: McGraw-Hill/Duskin.
Hester, T. R., R. F. Heizer, and J. A. Graham
   1975   *Field Methods in Archaeology*. 6th ed. Palo Alto: Mayfield Publishing
           Company.
Hickey, J.
   "An Archeological Survey of Charles County, Maryland." Master's thesis,
           George Washington University, Washington, D.C., 1970.
Hill, J.
   1968   "Broken K Pueblo: Patterns of Form and Function." In *New Per-
           spectives in Archeology*. Eds. L. R. Binford and S. R. Binford. Chica-
           go: Aldine Publishing Company, pp. 103–142.
   1970   "Broken K Pueblo: Prehistoric Social Organization in the Ameri-
           can Southwest." Anthropological papers of the Museum of An-
           thropology 18. Tucson, AZ: University of Arizona.
Hoebel, E. A.
   1966   *Anthropology: The Study of Man*. 3rd ed. New York: McGraw-Hill
           Book Company.
Hole, F., and R. F. Heizer.
   1975   *Introduction to Prehistoric Archaeology*. 4th ed. New York: Holt, Rine-
           hart and Winston.
Jackson, M. L.
   1958   *Soil Chemical Analysis*. New York: Prentice Hall.
Joukowsky, M.
   1981   *Complete Manual of Field Archaeology*. Englewood Cliffs, NJ: Prentice
           Hall.
Kamp, K.
   1998   *Life in the Pueblo: Understanding the Past through Archaeology*.
           Prospect Heights: Waveland Press.
Lee, R. B.
   1979   *The !Kung San: Men, Women, and Work in a Foraging Society*. New
           York: Cambridge University Press.

Longacre, W., and J. Ayres.
  1968   "Archeological Lessons from an Apache Wickiup." In *New Perspectives in Archeology*. Eds. S. Binford and L. Binford. Chicago: Aldine Publishing Company.
Malinowski, B.
  1922   *Argonauts of the Western Pacific*. New York: Dutton.
Matson, F., ed.
  1965   "Ceramics and Man." *Viking Fund Publications in Anthropology* 41 (New York).
McDowell, E. E.
  1968   "The Ruppert Island Site." Masters Thesis, The American University, Washington, D.C.
  1972   "A Techno-Ecological Model for the Study of the Archaic Stage of the Potomac River Piedmont." Doctoral dissertation, The American University, Washington, D.C.
McDowell-Loudan, E. E., and G. L. Loudan
  1993   *Report of the 1993 Archeological Study of 35 CO 30, Wyns Farm Site, Willet Quadrangle, Cortland County, New York*. Baltimore: United States Army Corps of Engineers, Baltimore District.
  1997   *The 1996 Archeological Study of 35 CO 30, Wyns Farm Site, Willet Quadrangle, Cortland County, New York*. Baltimore: United States Army Corps of Engineers, Baltimore District.
McGimsey, C. R., III.
  1972   *Public Archeology*. New York: Seminar Press.
  1994   "The Yin and Yang of Archaeology." *News Letter of the Society for Professional Archaeologists* 18, no. 10: 1–4.
McNett, C. W., Jr.
  1971   *The Inference of Socio-Cultural Traits in Archaeology: A Statistical Approach*. Ann Arbor, MI: University Microfilms, 68: 4056.
McNett, C. W., Jr., ed.
  1985   *Shawnee Minisink: A Stratified Paleoindian–Archaic Site in the Upper Delaware Valley of Pennsylvania*. Orlando: Harcourt Brace Jovanovich.
McNett, C. W., Jr., W. M. Gardner, and E. E. McDowell
  n.d.   "The Ruppert Island Site." On file. Washington, D.C.: The American University/Catholic University of America.
Meighan, C. W.
  1986   *Archaeology for Money*. Calabasas: Wormwood Press.
Messenger, P. M., ed.
  1987   *The Ethics of Collecting: Whose Culture? Cultural Property: Whose Property?* Albuquerque: University of New Mexico Press.
Mueller, J. W.
  1974   "The Use of Sampling in Archaeological Survey." Memoir 28. Washington, D.C.: Society for American Archaeology.

Oswalt, W. H., and J. W. Van Stone
  1967   "The Ethnoarchaeology of Crow Village, Alaska." *Smithsonian Institution Bulletins of American Ethnology* 199: 74–76.
Peregrine, P. M.
  2001   *Archaeological Research: A Brief Introduction.* Upper Saddle River, NJ: Prentice Hall.
Rathje, W.
  1979   "Modern Material Culture Studies." *Advances in Archaeological Method and Theory* 2: 1–37.
  1991   "Once and Future Landfills." *National Geographic* 179, no. 5: 116–134.
Rathje, W., and M. McCarthy
  1977   "Regularity and Variability in Contemporary Garbage." In *Research Strategies in Historical Archaeology.* Ed. S. South. New York: Academic Press.
Rathje, W., and C. Murphy.
  1992   *Rubbish: The Archaeology of Garbage.* New York: Harper Collins.
Register of Professional Archaeologists.
  2000   The Register: 2000–2001 Directory. Baltimore: Register of Professional Archaeologists.
Ritchie, W. A., and R. E. Funk.
  1973   "Aboriginal Settlement Patterns in the Northeast." Memoir 20. Albany: New York State Museum and Science Service.
Rupee, R.
  1966   "The Archaeological Survey: A Defense." *American Antiquity* 31: 313–333.
Semenov, S.
  1964   *Prehistoric Technology.* Trans. M. W. Thompson. London: Cory, Adams and MacKay.
Sheets, P.
  1992   *The Ceren Site: A Prehistoric Village Buried by Volcanic Ash in Central America.* Fort Worth, TX: Harcourt College Publishers.
Shepard, A.
  1956   "Ceramics for the Archaeologist." *Carnegie Institution of Washington Publications.*
Shostack, M.
  1981   *Nisa: The Life and Words of a !Kung Woman.* New York: Random House.
Taylor, W. W.
  1948   "A Study of Archaeology." Memoir 69. Washington, D.C.: American Anthropological Association.
Trubowitz, N.
  1973   "Controlled Surface Collection in Western New York State." Paper presented at Eastern States Archeological Federation.

Turnbaugh, W. A., R. Jurmain, H. Nelson, and L. Kilgore
  1999   *Understanding Physical Anthropology and Archaeology.* 7th ed. Belmont: West/Wadsworth.
U.S. Department of the Interior. National Park Service.
  n.d.   *Federal Archeology Report (Quarterly),* by Cultural Resources Departmental Consulting Archaeologists. Washington, D.C.: U.S. Government Printing Office.
Voegelin, E.
  1954   "Definition of Ethnohistory." *Ethnohistory* 1, no. 2: 166–171.
Watkins, Joe
  2000   "Writing Unwritten History." *Archaeology* (November/December).
  2000   *Indigenous Archaeology: American Indian Values and Scientific Practice.* Walnut Creek, CA: Altamira Press.
Webster, D., A. C. Freter, and N. Gonlin
  2000   *Copan: The Rise and Fall of an Ancient Maya Kingdom.* Fort Worth, TX: Harcourt College Publishers.
Weide, M. L.
  1975   "Research Design in Northeastern Prehistory." Paper presented at Society for American Archaeology, Dallas, TX.
Wheat, J. B.
  1967   "The Olsen-Chubbock Site: A Paleo-Indian Bison Kill." Memoir 26. Washington, D.C.: The Society for American Archaeology.
Wheeler, D.
  1998   "Archaeologists Use Technology to Avoid Invasive Excavations: Radar and Other Remote-Sensing Tools Can Guide Decisions about Where to Dig." In *Annual Editions Archaeology 00/01.* Sluice Dock, Guilford: Dushkin/McGraw-Hill, 2000. First published in *The Chronicle of Higher Education* (November 20): A13, A14.
Wheeler, M.
  1954   *Archaeology from the Earth.* Baltimore: Penguin Books.
Willey G., and P. Phillips
  1958   *Method and Theory in American Archaeology.* Chicago: University of Chicago Press.
Wilmsen, E.
  1968   "Paleo-Indian Site Utilization." In *Anthropological Archaeology in the Americas.* Ed. B. Meggers. Washington, D.C.: The Anthropological Society of Washington, D.C.
  1973   "Interaction, Spacing Behavior, and the Organization of Hunting Bands." *Journal of Anthropological Research* 29: 25–26.
  1974   *Lindenmeier: A Pleistocene Hunting Society.* New York: Harper and Row.
Woods, W.
  1975   "The Analysis of Abandoned Settlements by a New Phosphate Field Test Method." *The Chesopiean Journal of Science* (Norfolk).

INDEX

Note: Page numbers in italics refer to illustrations on that page.